The Literacy and Numeracy Song Book

Edited by
Gerald Haigh and Peter Morrell

London

© 1998 **p**fp publishing ltd
© in all songs rests with the writers as credited

First published in Britain in 1998 by
pfp publishing ltd
61 Gray's Inn Rd
London
WC1X 8TL

Printed in the UK

All rights reserved. No part of this publication may be reproduced, stored in a retrieval system, copied or transmitted without the permission of the publisher except that the music and words may be photocopied for use in the purchasing institution only without seeking permission from the publisher.

The authors assert their moral right to be identified as the authors of this work.

ISBN 1 874050 41 4

A catalogue record for this book is available from the British Library.

THE LITERACY AND NUMERACY SONG BOOK

Contents

	writer	CD disc–track melody/acc.	page
Editorial and Acknowledgements			5

Literacy Songs

Adjectives
The Adjective Song	Susan Eames	1–1/2	6
Adjectivally Me	Clive Barnwell	1–3/4	9

Adverbs
The Adverb Song	Peter Morrell	1–5/6	12

Language
The Opposites Gang	Susan Eames	1–7/8	15
A, E, I, O and U	Susan Eames	1–9/10 *version A*	17
		1–11/12 *version B*	

Reading
I Love Those Fairy Tales	Hazel Hobbs	1–13/14	20
When I Look in a Book	Johanne Levy	1–15/16	23
Read All About It!	Hazel Hobbs	1–17/18	26
Fact or Opinion?	Clive Barnwell	1–19/20	29

Spelling
Magic E	Susan Eames	1–21/22	32
Look, Cover, Write and Check It	Susan Eames	1–23/24	35
I Before E	Susan Eames	1–25/26	38
A Sound Song	Clive Barnwell	1–27/28	41
The H Song	Clive Barnwell	1–29/30	44

Story–Telling
Puss in Boots Rap	Susan Eames	1–31/32	47

Writing
Apostrophes	Susan Eames	1–33/34	50
Do They Ride into the Sun?	Clive Barnwell	1–35/36	54
Punctuation Signs	Susan Eames	1–37/38	57
The Writing's on the Wall	Peter Morrell	1–39/40	60
Similes	Clive Barnwell	1–41/42	64
Capital Letter Blues	Peter Morrell	1–43/44	67

© pfp publishing ltd 1998 • ISBN 1 874050 41 4
May be photocopied for use only within the purchasing institution
pfp 61 Gray's Inn Road London WC1X 8TL

THE LITERACY AND NUMERACY SONG BOOK

Numeracy Songs

	writer	CD disc–track melody/acc.	page
Addition			
Dinosaurs	Susan Eames	2–1/2	73
Ten Fat Caterpillars	Susan Eames	2–3/4	76
Angles			
Cutting Corners	Maurice Walsh	2–5/6	79
Counting			
One Knock at the Door	Johanne Levy	2–7/8	82
Cornucopia	Jean Gilbert	2–9/10	85
Count Your Fingers	Johanne Levy	2–11/12	88
Division			
Sausage Boogie	Gerald Haigh	2–13/14	90
Sharing	Susan Eames	2–15/16	94
Twenty-Four Pieces – Wow!	Maurice Walsh	2–17/18	96
Measurement			
Peter Metre Eater	David Moses	2–19/20	100
Multiplication			
Multiplication March	Maurice Walsh	2–21/22	103
Soldiers Marching	Susan Eames	2–23/24	105
The Seven Times Table Song	Maurice Walsh	2–25/26	108
Numbers			
Number Blues	Hazel Hobbs	2–27/28	111
Day without Numbers	Hazel Hobbs	2–29/30	114
Clementine	Belinda Morley	2–31/32	117
Positions			
Up, Down, Round About	Maurice Walsh	2–33/34	119
Shapes			
Sir Cumference	Clive Barnwell	2–35/36	122
Symmetry	Maurice Walsh	2–37/38	125
Plane Shapes and Solids	Maurice Walsh	2–39/40	127
Subtraction			
Octopus Tea	Maurice Walsh	2–41/42	129
Ten Little Children	Susan Eames	2–43/44	132
Time			
The Clock Song	Clive Barnwell	2–45/46	135
Passing Time	Gerald Haigh	2–47/48	139
Notes for Teachers			141

Editorial and Acknowledgements

The **Literacy and Numeracy Song Book** responds to a wish, expressed by many primary teachers, for songs which will support the teaching of literacy and numeracy. Primary teachers know that rhyme, rhythm and music work together to help words and ideas to stay in the memory, which is why they use jingles and songs in lessons right across the curriculum.

We hope that teachers will use this book within literacy and numeracy lessons not only to add immediate reinforcement to particular teaching points but to add colour, variety and enjoyment – perhaps to round off a concentrated session with something less demanding. Many of the songs are, of course, also suitable for assembly, as well as being capable of finding a place in the music curriculum itself.

The songs are divided into two strands – Literacy and Numeracy. Within each of these there are groups of songs corresponding to some of the main teaching topics.

The Notes for Teachers indicate an age range for each song, though this is a guide only and teachers will make their own judgments based on their classroom experience.

A note on the music

The piano score has been written for the busy non-specialist, with little time for practise. An accomplished pianist will find it easy to add to what is written.

The guitar chord symbols will also be useful to a pianist or keyboard player. A chord symbol occasionally describes a slightly simpler chord than is notated in the piano score, but in these cases the two chords will work well together.

About the CD

For each song the CD provides the following.
- The melody only, played on a piano. This is intended to provide help in learning the song.
- A full piano performance of the song with all verses. This will also help with learning, but can also be used as an accompaniment if no pianist is available.

The piano performance is not an exact reproduction of the printed score, because the pianist provides the kind of embellishment that a resourceful musician will typically add to what is printed. However, the melodies and the underlying harmonic and rhythmic structures are always faithful to the printed page. Experience with pfp's **Primary Assembly Song Book** has shown that even the most accomplished classroom musician will pick up some musical ideas from the CD.

Using the CD for teaching

Ideally, you will first learn the song yourself and then teach it by singing it to the children, using the CD for support and reinforcement.

When you use the CD to teach a song, either to yourself or to the children, use both the melody line version and the full version, moving between them as necessary. The melody line makes the tune clear, but you really need to hear the full version to make sense of the harmonic and rhythmic structure.

Notes and acknowledgments

Many thanks are due to the song writers. They have responded with imagination and creativity to the challenge of providing songs which support the curriculum as well as being fun to sing. We owe thanks, too, to Phil Alexander who helped interpret the writers' work and who arranged and performed the recorded versions on the accompanying CDs.

Gerald Haigh and **Peter Morrell** are both former Warwickshire teachers with a shared interest in school music making. Both have long experience of writing and editing children's songs.

Clive Barnwell is a primary teacher who has written many songs and musical plays for children.

Debbie Campbell is a music teacher and composer with a special interest in youth music theatre.

Susan Eames is an experienced primary school teacher whose songs, poems and stories have been published in various collections.

Jean Gilbert has taught across the whole age range, and has written and co-written many resource books, including the *Oxford Music Scheme*.

Hazel Hobbs is a primary school teacher who has had numerous songs published and has responsibility for music at her present school.

Johanne Levy teaches piano, guitar and clarinet, and has published many songs and instrumental pieces for a wide age range.

David Moses is a composer, author and freelance performer who was previously Head of Music at Lewisham College.

Maurice Walsh is a teacher with the Manchester Music Service. He contributed many songs to the widely used Manchester Music Programme for primary schools.

The Adjective Song

ADJECTIVES

THE ADJECTIVE SONG

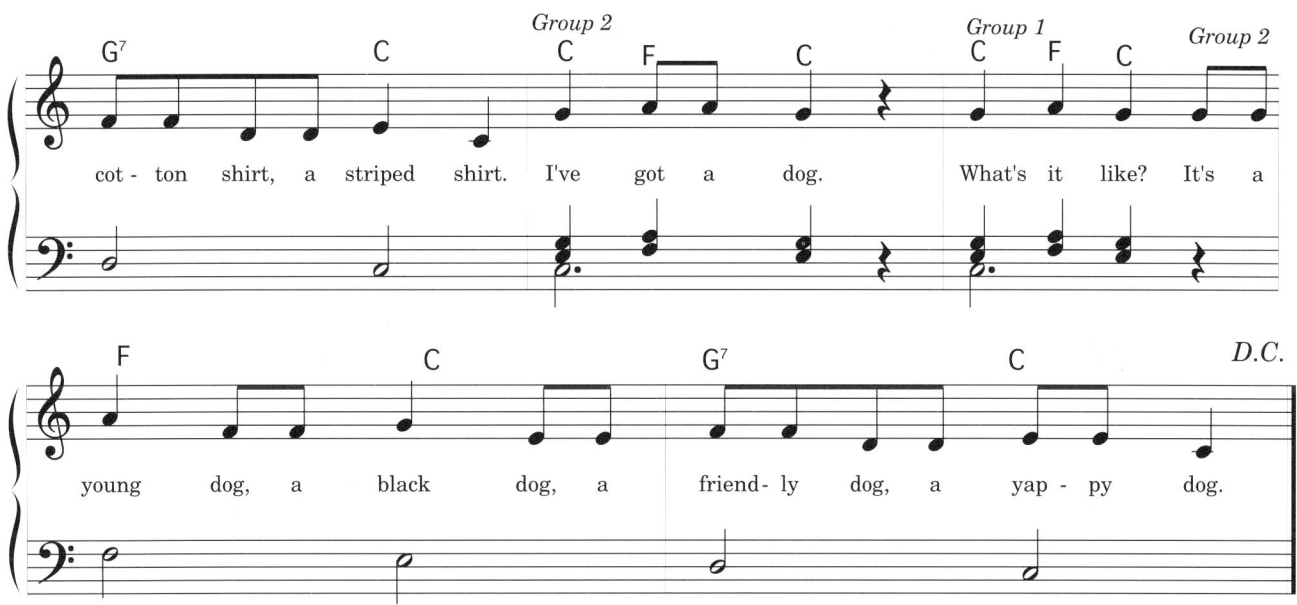

Chorus
An adjective, an adjective,
A very useful adjective,
Tells you more about a noun.
An adjective, an adjective,
A very useful adjective,
Tells you about a person,
An animal, place or thing.

Verse
I've got a shirt.
What's it like?
It's a new shirt, a red shirt,
A cotton shirt, a striped shirt.
I've got a dog.
What's it like?
It's a young dog, a black dog,
A friendly dog, a yappy dog.

Chorus

The Adjective Song

Chorus
An adjective, an adjective,
A very useful adjective,
Tells you more about a noun.
An adjective, an adjective,
A very useful adjective,
Tells you about a person,
An animal, place or thing.

Verse
I've got a shirt.
What's it like?
It's a new shirt, a red shirt,
A cotton shirt, a striped shirt.
I've got a dog.
What's it like?
It's a young dog, a black dog,
A friendly dog, a yappy dog.

Chorus

Adjectivally Me!

Clive Barnwell

ADJECTIVALLY ME!

ADJECTIVES

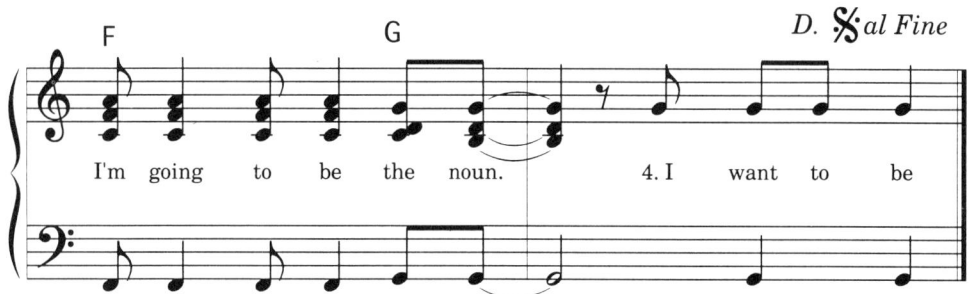

1.
I want to be happy, rich and funny.
I want to be loud and quiet too.
And if you can find any word to describe me with,
That is an adjective.

2.
I want to be friendly, kind and clever.
I want to be patient and be true.
And if you can find any word to describe me with,
That is an adjective.

3.
I need to be hopeful and contented.
I need to be honest, true and sound.
And if you find adjectives that'll suit me well,
I'm going to be the noun.

4.
I want to be golden, bright and sunny.
I want to be smart and fresh and new.
And if you can find any word to describe me with,
That is an adjective.

Adjectivally Me!

1.
I want to be happy, rich and funny.
I want to be loud and quiet too.
And if you can find any word to describe me with,
That is an adjective.

2.
I want to be friendly, kind and clever.
I want to be patient and be true.
And if you can find any word to describe me with,
That is an adjective.

3.
I need to be hopeful and contented.
I need to be honest, true and sound.
And if you find adjectives that'll suit me well,
I'm going to be the noun.

4.
I want to be golden, bright and sunny.
I want to be smart and fresh and new.
And if you can find any word to describe me with,
That is an adjective.

The Adverb Song

Peter Morrell

ADVERBS

THE ADVERB SONG

1.
Oh, let's see how we run today,
Slowly, quickly, come what may.
This way, that way, just you say,
And that's how we run today.

2.
Oh, let's see how we walk today,
Briskly, dreamily, come what may.
This way, that way, just you say,
And that's how we walk today.

3.
Oh, let's see how we creep today,
Stealthily, silently, come what may.
This way, that way, just you say,
And that's how we creep today.

4.
Oh, let's see how we jump today,
Heavily, lightly, come what may.
This way, that way, just you say.
And that's how we jump today.

5.
Oh, let's see how we eat today,
Hungrily, politely, come what may.
This way, that way, just you say,
And that's how we eat today.

6.
Oh, let's see how we play today,
Noisily, energetically, come what may.
This way, that way, just you say,
And that's how we play today.

7.
Oh, let's see how we work today,
Quietly, enjoyably, come what may.
This way, that way, just you say,
And that's how we work today.

8.
Oh, let's see how we laugh today,
Loudly, continuously, come what may.
This way, that way, just you say,
And that's how we laugh today.

9.
Oh, let's see how we write today,
Hurriedly, beautifully, come what may.
This way, that way, just you say,
And that's how we write today.

The Adverb Song

1.
Oh, let's see how we run today,
Slowly, quickly, come what may.
This way, that way, just you say,
And that's how we run today.

2.
Oh, let's see how we walk today,
Briskly, dreamily, come what may.
This way, that way, just you say,
And that's how we walk today.

3.
Oh, let's see how we creep today,
Stealthily, silently, come what may.
This way, that way, just you say,
And that's how we creep today.

4.
Oh, let's see how we jump today,
Heavily, lightly, come what may.
This way, that way, just you say,
And that's how we jump today.

5.
Oh, let's see how we eat today,
Hungrily, politely, come what may.
This way, that way, just you say,
And that's how we eat today.

6.
Oh, let's see how we play today,
Noisily, energetically, come what may.
This way, that way, just you say,
And that's how we play today.

7.
Oh, let's see how we work today,
Quietly, enjoyably, come what may.
This way, that way, just you say,
And that's how we work today.

8.
Oh, let's see how we laugh today,
Loudly, continuously, come what may.
This way, that way, just you say,
And that's how we laugh today.

9.
Oh, let's see how we write today,
Hurriedly, beautifully, come what may.
This way, that way, just you say,
And that's how we write today.

LANGUAGE THE OPPOSITES GANG

The Opposites Gang

Susan Eames

Chorus
We're the Opposites Gang,
We're the Opposites Gang,
And we never, never are the same,
And we never, never are the same.

1. I'm big!
   I'm small!
   I'm short!
   I'm tall!

Chorus

2. I'm young!
   I'm old!
   I'm hot!
   I'm cold!

Chorus

3. I'm out!
   I'm in!
   I'm fat!
   I'm thin!

Chorus

4. I'm high!
   I'm low!
   I come!
   I go!

© pfp publishing ltd 1998 • ISBN 1 874050 41 4
May be photocopied for use only within the purchasing institution
pfp 61 Gray's Inn Road London WC1X 8TL

The Opposites Gang

Chorus
We're the Opposites Gang,
We're the Opposites Gang,
And we never, never are the same,
And we never, never are the same.

1. I'm big!
   I'm small!
   I'm short!
   I'm tall!

Chorus

2. I'm young!
   I'm old!
   I'm hot!
   I'm cold!

Chorus

3. I'm out!
   I'm in!
   I'm fat!
   I'm thin!

Chorus

4. I'm high!
   I'm low!
   I come!
   I go!

LANGUAGE

A, E, I, O and U

Susan Eames

A, E, I, O AND U

LANGUAGE

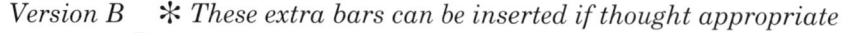

Version B ✱ *These extra bars can be inserted if thought appropriate*

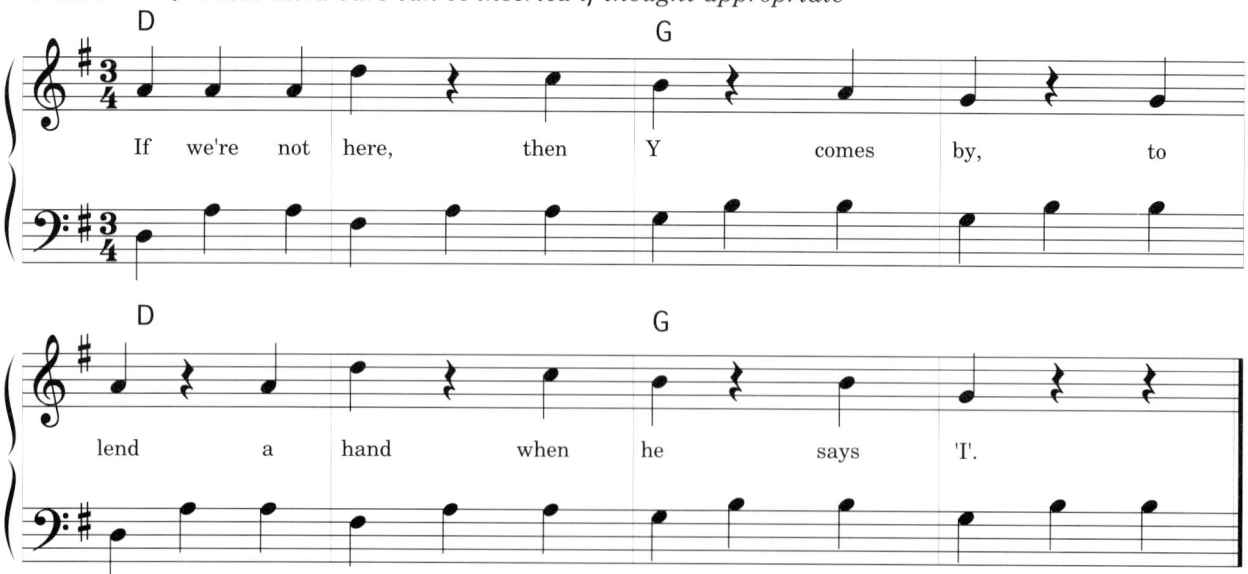

Version A
A, E, I, O and U.
We're very important letters.
A, E, I, O and U.
So never, never forget us.
In the alphabet we are few.
We're the vowels who work for you.✱
A, E, I, O and U.
We're vowels so never forget us.

✱ *Version B. These extra words can be inserted if thought appropriate:*

If we're not here, then Y comes by
To lend a hand when he says 'I'.

A, E, I, O and U

Version A

A, E, I, O and U.
We're very important letters.
A, E, I, O and U.
So never, never forget us.
In the alphabet we are few.
We're the vowels who work for you.
A, E, I, O and U.
We're vowels so never forget us.

Version B

A, E, I, O and U.
We're very important letters.
A, E, I, O and U.
So never, never forget us.
In the alphabet we are few.
We're the vowels who work for you.
If we're not here, then Y comes by
To lend a hand when he says 'I'.
A, E, I, O and U.
We're vowels so never forget us.

I Love Those Fairy Tales

Hazel Hobbs

READING

I LOVE THOSE FAIRY TALES

The giants, the dragons, the witches, the ghosties,
  they scare me.
The monsters, the goblins, the wicked wizards
  and fairies.
But I can't close the book 'til I reach the end.
I'm frightened but I need to read to the end.
Imagining one of the characters is me,
That's my favourite fantasy.
The giants, the dragons, the witches, the ghosties,
  they scare me.
The monsters, the goblins, I love those fairy tales.

I Love Those Fairy Tales

The giants, the dragons, the witches, the ghosties,
 they scare me.
The monsters, the goblins, the wicked wizards
 and fairies.
But I can't close the book 'til I reach the end.
I'm frightened but I need to read to the end.
Imagining one of the characters is me,
That's my favourite fantasy.
The giants, the dragons, the witches, the ghosties,
 they scare me.
The monsters, the goblins, I love those fairy tales.

When I Look in a Book

Johanne Levy

WHEN I LOOK IN A BOOK

READING

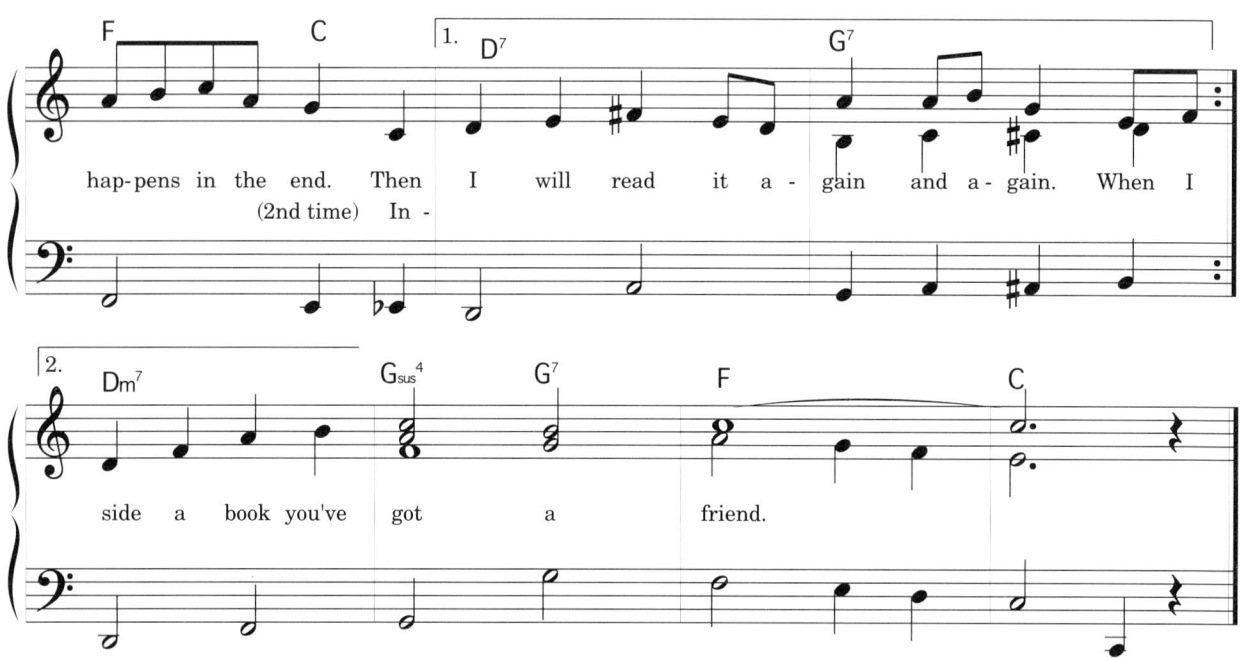

Chorus
When I look in a book
At the words on a page,
There's so much I can see to excite me.
For I know in those words,
In those letters on a page,
There's a story to delight me.

1.
Every single letter, every single word,
Will light up my life with a story.
I can't wait to read what happens in the end.
Then I will read it again and again.

Chorus

2.
As I turn the pages, pictures in my mind
Will light up my life with a story.
I can't wait to read what happens in the end.
Inside a book you've got a friend.

When I Look in a Book

Chorus
When I look in a book
At the words on a page,
There's so much I can see to excite me.
For I know in those words,
In those letters on a page,
There's a story to delight me.

1.
Every single letter, every single word,
Will light up my life with a story.
I can't wait to read what happens in the end.
Then I will read it again and again.

Chorus

2.
As I turn the pages, pictures in my mind
Will light up my life with a story.
I can't wait to read what happens in the end.
Inside a book you've got a friend.

Read All About It!

Hazel Hobbs

READING — READ ALL ABOUT IT!

1.
'Where's the morning paper?'
Is the daily cry at our house.
Everybody wants to read the news.
Where's 'The Mirror'?
From the front page scandal
To the back page sports reports,
World events and video reviews.

Chorus
Read all about it, read all about it,
Read all about it in the daily paper.
Read all about it, read all about it,
Read all about the latest news.

2.
Have you seen the paper?
Is the magazine inside it?
Everybody wants to read a page.
Where's 'The Mirror'?
Have you done the crossword puzzle?
Where's the TV guide?
Who's appearing on the theatre stage?

Chorus

3.
Check the fashion pages.
Have you seen the latest hairstyle?
Readers' letters make me want to swear!
Where's 'The Mirror'?
Wonder what the forecast is
For weather here today?
Where's the page that shows the stocks
   and shares?

Chorus

THE LITERACY AND NUMERACY SONG BOOK

Read All About It!

1. 'Where's the morning paper?'
   Is the daily cry at our house.
   Everybody wants to read the news
   Where's 'The Mirror'?
   From the front page scandal
   To the back page sports reports,
   World events and video reviews.

Chorus
Read all about it, read all about it,
Read all about it in the daily paper.
Read all about it, read all about it,
Read all about the latest news.

2. Have you seen the paper?
   Is the magazine inside it?
   Everybody wants to read a page.
   Where's 'The Mirror'?
   Have you done the crossword puzzle?
   Where's the TV guide?
   Who's appearing on the theatre stage?

Chorus

3. Check the fashion pages.
   Have you seen the latest hairstyle?
   Readers' letters make me want to swear!
   Where's 'The Mirror'?
   Wonder what the forecast is
   For weather here today?
   Where's the page that shows the stocks and shares?

Chorus

Fact or Opinion?

Clive Barnwell

FACT OR OPINION?

READING

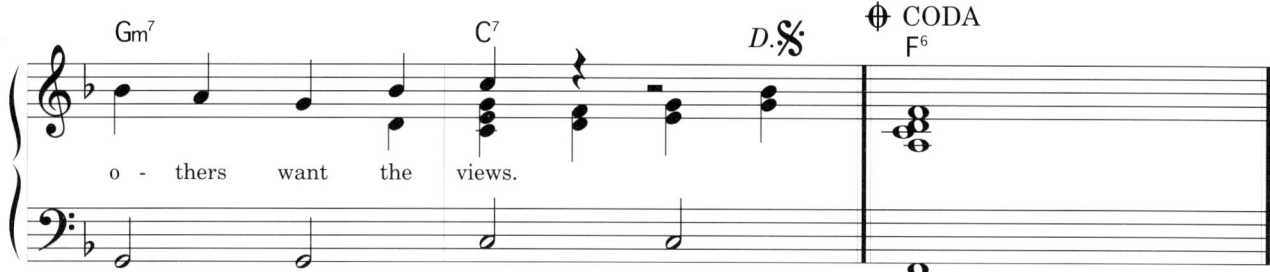

Is it fact? Is it opinion?
Man, eighteen, wins a half of a million.
Hopes to fly to somewhere Brazilian.
Is it fact or is it opinion?

Is it fact? Is it opinion?
This year's colours are peach and
  vermilion.
Favourite name for girls will be Lillian.
Is it fact or is it opinion?

All over the world.
Any language you choose.
There's people who want the facts
And others want the views.

Is it fact? Is it opinion?
Newly weds hire a cricket pavilion.
He's a soldier. She's a civilian.
Is it fact or is it opinion?

Is it fact? Is it opinion?
All the best sorts of pets are reptilian.
'Specially if they're Greek or Sicilian.
Is it fact or is it opinion?

All over the world.
Any language you choose.
There's people who want the facts
And others want the views.

Is it fact? Is it opinion?
Man, eighteen, wins a half of a million.
Hopes to fly to somewhere Brazilian.
Is it fact or is it opinion?

Fact or Opinion?

Is it fact? Is it opinion?
Man, eighteen, wins a half of a million.
Hopes to fly to somewhere Brazilian.
Is it fact or is it opinion?

Is it fact? Is it opinion?
This year's colours are peach and vermilion.
Favourite name for girls will be Lillian.
Is it fact or is it opinion?

All over the world.
Any language you choose.
There's people who want the facts
And others want the views.

Is it fact? Is it opinion?
Newly weds hire a cricket pavilion.
He's a soldier. She's a civilian.
Is it fact or is it opinion?

Is it fact? Is it opinion?
All the best sorts of pets are reptilian.
'Specially if they're Greek or Sicilian.
Is it fact or is it opinion?

All over the world.
Any language you choose.
There's people who want the facts
And others want the views.

Is it fact? Is it opinion?
Man, eighteen, wins a half of a million.
Hopes to fly to somewhere Brazilian.
Is it fact or is it opinion?

Magic E

Susan Eames

SPELLING MAGIC E

1.
Magic E, Magic E
Makes vowels say their name.
Magic E, Magic E
Makes vowels say their name.
It makes pin pine,
It makes fin fine,
It makes bit bite,
It makes kit kite.
It makes mat mate,
It makes hat hate.
It's magic, can't you see?
Magic E, Magic E,
Clever Magic E.

2.
Magic E, Magic E
Makes vowels say their name.
Magic E, Magic E
Makes vowels say their name.
It makes can cane,
It makes man mane,
It makes cub cube,
It makes tub tube.
It makes hid hide,
It makes Sid side.
It's magic, can't you see?
Magic E, Magic E,
Clever Magic E.

Magic E

1.
Magic E, Magic E
Makes vowels say *their* name.
Magic E, Magic E
Makes vowels say *their* name.
It makes pin pine,
It makes fin fine,
It makes bit bite,
It makes kit kite.
It makes mat mate,
It makes hat hate.
It's magic, can't you see?
Magic E, Magic E,
Clever Magic E.

2.
Magic E, Magic E
Makes vowels say *their* name.
Magic E, Magic E
Makes vowels say *their* name.
It makes can cane,
It makes man mane,
It makes cub cube,
It makes tub tube.
It makes hid hide,
It makes Sid side.
It's magic, can't you see?
Magic E, Magic E,
Clever Magic E.

Look, Cover, Write and Check It

Susan Eames

LOOK, COVER, WRITE AND CHECK IT

SPELLING

1.
Here's a good strategy for learning to spell a word.
It could be the best plan you have ever heard.

Look, cover, write and check it.
Look, cover, write and check it.
Remember this plan and you'll not regret it.
Look, cover, write and check it.

2.
Here's a good plan if you want to learn each letter.
A plan worth trying, I don't know one that's better.

Look, cover, write and check it.
Look, cover, write and check it.
Remember this plan and you'll not regret it.
Look, cover, write and check it.
(Spoken) Look, cover, write and check it.

Look, Cover, Write and Check It

1.
Here's a good strategy for learning to spell a word.
It could be the best plan you have ever heard.

Look, cover, write and check it.
Look, cover, write and check it.
Remember this plan and you'll not regret it.
Look, cover, write and check it.

2.
Here's a good plan if you want to learn each letter.
A plan worth trying, I don't know one that's better.

Look, cover, write and check it.
Look, cover, write and check it.
Remember this plan and you'll not regret it.
Look, cover, write and check it.
(Spoken) Look, cover, write and check it.

I Before E

Susan Eames

SPELLING I BEFORE E

came to grief when he hid a sto-len shield in a far-mer's field. rule. 2. So re-mem-ber you'll ne-ver be-lieve what you can a-chieve 'til you fol-low this brief piece of ad-vice.

CODA
that's the rule.

Chorus
I before E except after C,
In spelling a good rule for you and for me.
I, E, but not after C,
That's the rule.

So remember the chief thief who came to grief
When he hid a stolen shield in a farmer's field.

Chorus

So remember you'll never believe what
 you can achieve
'Til you follow this brief piece of advice.

Chorus

I Before E

Chorus
I before E except after C,
In spelling a good rule for you and for me.
I, E, but not after C,
That's the rule.

1.
So remember the chief thief who came to grief
When he hid a stolen shield in a farmer's field.

Chorus

2.
So remember you'll never believe what you can achieve
'Til you follow this brief piece of advice.

Chorus

A Sound Song

Clive Barnwell

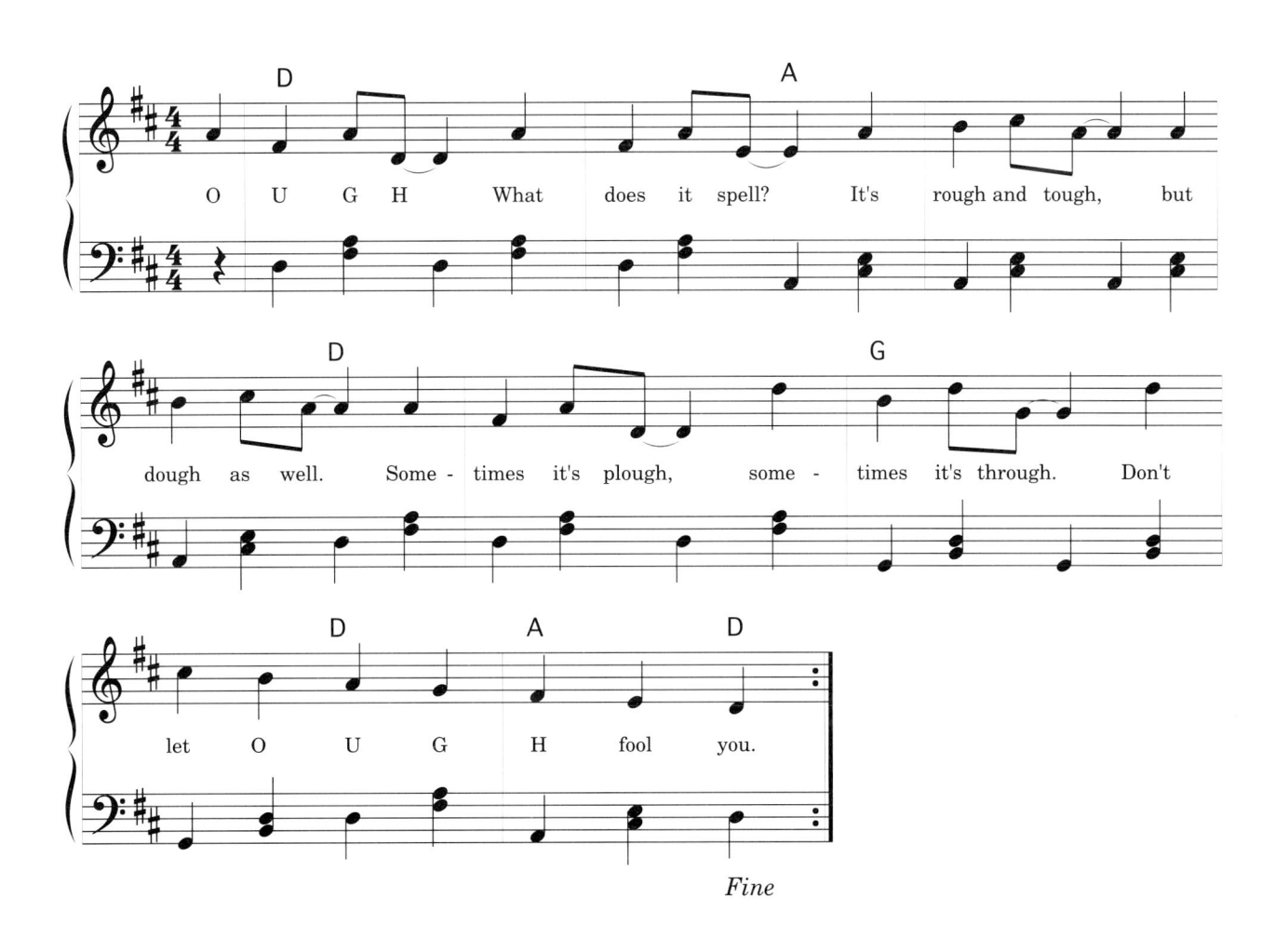

O U G H What does it spell? It's rough and tough, but dough as well. Sometimes it's plough, sometimes it's through. Don't let O U G H fool you.

Fine

A SOUND SONG

1.
O U G H
What does it spell?
It's rough and tough,
But dough as well.
Sometimes it's plough.
Sometimes it's through.
Don't let O U G H fool you.

2.
I G H T
What does it spell?
A sight that's light
And bright as well.
It comes at night
And in flight too.
Don't let I G H T fool you.

3.
T I O N
What does it spell?
In lotions and
Potions as well.
In fractions and
In stations too.
Don't let T I O N fool you.

4.
E I G H
What does it spell?
It's there in weigh
And sleigh as well.
Each horse's neigh
And eighty-two.
Don't let E I G H fool you.

A Sound Song

1.
O U G H
What does it spell?
It's rough and tough,
But dough as well.
Sometimes it's plough.
Sometimes it's through.
Don't let O U G H fool you.

2.
I G H T
What does it spell?
A sight that's light
And bright as well.
It comes at night
And in flight too.
Don't let I G H T fool you.

3.
T I O N
What does it spell?
In lotions and
Potions as well.
In fractions and
In stations too.
Don't let T I O N fool you.

4.
E I G H
What does it spell?
It's there in weigh
And sleigh as well.
Each horse's neigh
And eighty-two.
Don't let E I G H fool you.

The H Song

Clive Barnwell

I can go with C and I go ch, ch, ch. C and H to-ge-ther they go ch, ch, ch. If the H should ev-er be be-side the let-ter C, then they fin-ish up to-ge-ther go-ing ch, ch, ch, ch, ch.

th.

SPELLING

THE H SONG

1.
I can go with C and I go ch, ch, ch.
C and H together they go ch, ch, ch.
If the H should ever be
Beside the letter C,
Then they finish up together going ch, ch, ch, ch, ch.

2.
I can go with T and I go th, th, th.
T and H together they go th, th, th.
If the H should ever be
Beside the letter T,
Then they finish up together going th, th, th, th, th.

3.
I can go with P and I go ph, ph, ph.
P and H together they go ph, ph, ph.
If the H should ever be
Beside the letter P,
Then they finish up together going ph, ph, ph, ph, ph.

4.
I can go with S and I go sh, sh, sh.
S and H together they go sh, sh, sh.
If the H should ever be
Beside the letter S,
Then they finish up together going sh, sh, sh, sh, sh.

The H Song

1.
I can go with C and I go ch, ch, ch.
C and H together they go ch, ch, ch.
If the H should ever be
Beside the letter C,
Then they finish up together going ch, ch, ch, ch, ch.

2.
I can go with T and I go th, th, th.
T and H together they go th, th, th.
If the H should ever be
Beside the letter T,
Then they finish up together going th, th, th, th, th.

3.
I can go with P and I go ph, ph, ph.
P and H together they go ph, ph, ph.
If the H should ever be
Beside the letter P,
Then they finish up together going ph, ph, ph, ph, ph.

4.
I can go with S and I go sh, sh, sh.
S and H together they go sh, sh, sh.
If the H should ever be
Beside the letter S,
Then they finish up together going sh, sh, sh, sh, sh.

Puss in Boots Rap

Susan Eames

I'm Puss in Boots, I'm a clever cat. I live with the Miller's son, fancy that!

(To rap, then repeat chorus)

Verse 1
The miller's son was a poor young man and so to help I devised a plan. He went for a swim and I hid his clothes. He'd nothing to wear, from his head to his toes.

Verse 2
A coach came past, with a princess inside. "Here's clothes," said the king, "and we'll give you a ride". I ran in front, I went ahead to an ogre's castle, and this is what I said.

PUSS IN BOOTS RAP

Verse 3

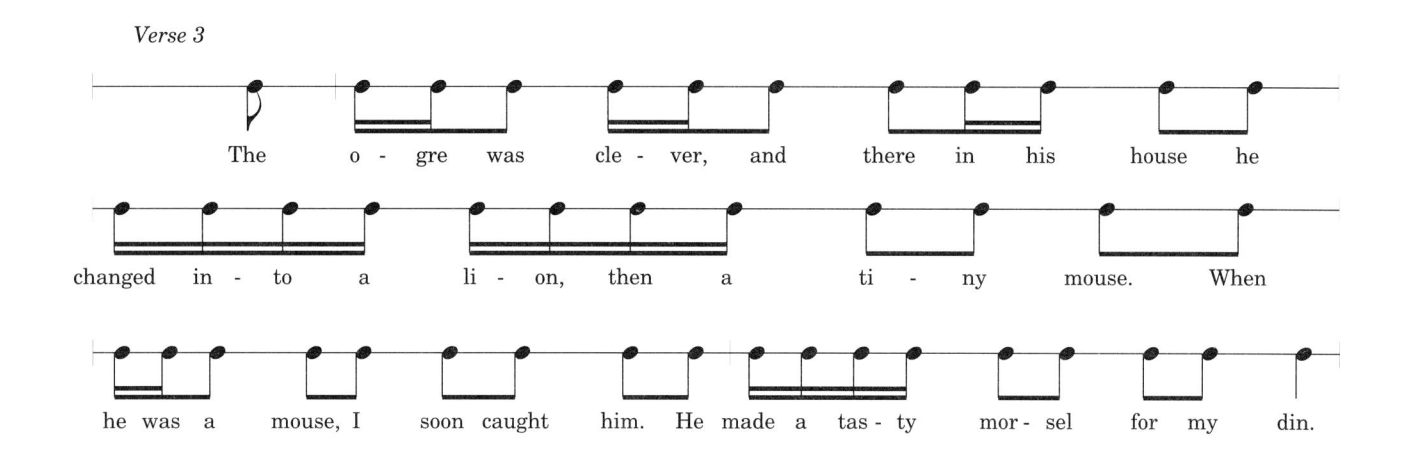

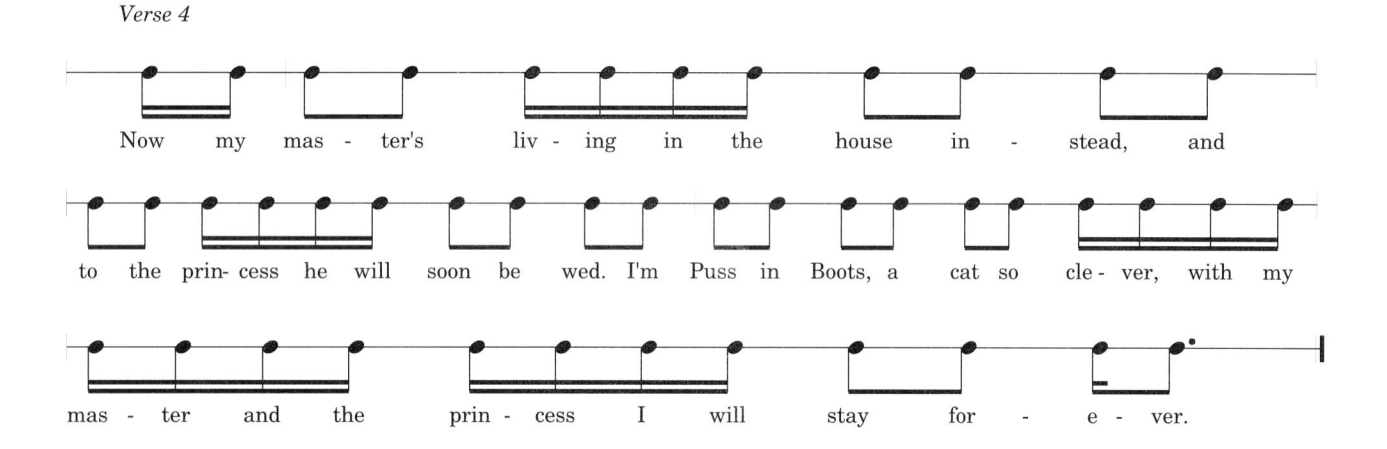

The o-gre was cle-ver, and there in his house he changed in-to a li-on, then a ti-ny mouse. When he was a mouse, I soon caught him. He made a tas-ty mor-sel for my din.

Verse 4

Now my mas-ter's liv-ing in the house in-stead, and to the prin-cess he will soon be wed. I'm Puss in Boots, a cat so cle-ver, with my mas-ter and the prin-cess I will stay for-e-ver.

Chorus
I'm Puss in Boots, I'm a clever cat.
I live with the miller's son, fancy that!

1.
The miller's son was a poor young man
And so to help I devised a plan.
He went for a swim and I hid his clothes.
He'd nothing to wear, from his head to his toes.

Chorus

2.
A coach came past, with a princess inside.
"Here's clothes" said the king "and we'll give you a ride".
I ran in front, I went ahead,
To an ogre's castle, and this is what I said.

Chorus

3.
The ogre was clever, and there in his house
He changed into a lion, then a tiny mouse.
When he was a mouse, I soon caught him.
He made a tasty morsel for my din.

Chorus

4.
Now my master's living in the house instead,
And to the princess he will soon be wed.
I'm Puss in Boots, a cat so clever,
With my master and princess I will stay forever.

Chorus

Puss in Boots Rap

Chorus
I'm Puss in Boots, I'm a clever cat.
I live with the miller's son, fancy that!

1.
The miller's son was a poor young man
And so to help I devised a plan.
He went for a swim and I hid his clothes.
He'd nothing to wear, from his head to his toes.

Chorus

2.
A coach came past, with a princess inside.
"Here's clothes" said the king "and we'll give you a ride".
I ran in front, I went ahead,
To an ogre's castle, and this is what I said.

Chorus

3.
The ogre was clever, and there in his house
He changed into a lion, then a tiny mouse.
When he was a mouse, I soon caught him.
He made a tasty morsel for my din.

Chorus

4.
Now my master's living in the house instead,
And to the princess he will soon be wed.
I'm Puss in Boots, a cat so clever,
With my master and princess I will stay forever.

Chorus

Apostrophes

Susan Eames

WRITING
APOSTOPHES

...all over the place.

1. In bananas in the shops, their trespass never stops. In apples and in pears, you can catch them unawares. But if the apostrophe be gone! You're not needed here. Get out! Get out! Get Out! *(spoken)*

2. They fill in for missing letters, as in he's and she's and that's. They tell us who possesses what, like "This is Steven's hat". If the S means more than one, then apostrophe be gone! You're not needed here. Get out! Get out! Get Out!

APOSTROPHES

Chorus
Apostrophes, apostrophes, they're all over the place.
Apostrophes, apostrophes, it really is a disgrace.
The way that they get in when they're not needed,
The way they get around when they're not heeded,
It really is a disgrace!

1.
Apostrophes, apostrophes, they're all over the place.
In bananas in the shops, their trespass never stops.
In apples and in pears, you can catch them unawares.
If the S means more than one, then apostrophe be gone!
You're not needed here. Get out! Get out!
(Spoken) Get out!

Chorus

2.
Apostrophes, apostrophes, they're all over the place.
They fill in for missing letters, as in he's and she's and that's.
They tell us who possesses what, like 'This is Steven's hat'.
But if the S means more than one, then apostrophe be gone!
You're not needed here. Get out! Get out!
(Spoken) Get out!

Apostrophes

Chorus
Apostrophes, apostrophes, they're all over the place.
Apostrophes, apostrophes, it really is a disgrace.
The way that they get in when they're not needed,
The way they get around when they're not heeded,
It really is a disgrace!

1.
Apostrophes, apostrophes, they're all over the place.
In bananas in the shops, their trespass never stops.
In apples and in pears, you can catch them unawares.
If the S means more than one, then apostrophe be gone!
You're not needed here. Get out! Get out!
(Spoken) Get out!

Chorus

2.
Apostrophes, apostrophes, they're all over the place.
They fill in for missing letters, as in he's and she's and that's.
They tell us who possesses what, like 'This is Steven's hat'.
But if the S means more than one, then apostrophe be gone!
You're not needed here. Get out! Get out!
(Spoken) Get out!

Do They Ride into the Sun?

Clive Barnwell

Ev'ry story has a start. And the middle is the part
not until the end of a world of pure pretend,
where the action starts to move and starts to grow.
that the story tells you what you want to know.
But it's
And do they
ride into the sun, or do they have to leave and run?
face what danger sends? End up as enemies or friends?

WRITING — DO THEY RIDE INTO THE SUN?

Every story has a start
And the middle is the part
Where the action starts to move and starts to grow.

But it's not until the end
Of a world of pure pretend
That the story tells you what you want to know.

And do they ride into the sun?
Or do they have to leave and run?
Do things turn out alright?
You'll find out when the story's done.

And do they face what danger sends?
End up as enemies or friends?
Or do they lose the fight?
You'll find out when the story ends.

Do They Ride into the Sun?

Every story has a start
And the middle is the part
Where the action starts to move and starts to grow.

But it's not until the end
Of a world of pure pretend
That the story tells you what you want to know.

And do they ride into the sun?
Or do they have to leave and run?
Do things turn out alright?
You'll find out when the story's done.

And do they face what danger sends?
End up as enemies or friends?
Or do they lose the fight?
You'll find out when the story ends.

Punctuation Signs

Susan Eames

Chorus
As you jour-ney through each sen-tence, signs will help you on your way. As you jour-ney through each sen-tence, punc-tu-a-tion signs will help you on your way.

Slower
Verse
Watch out for the small-est sign, its spe-cial mess-age send when you've writt-en down a sen-tence, put a full stop at the end.

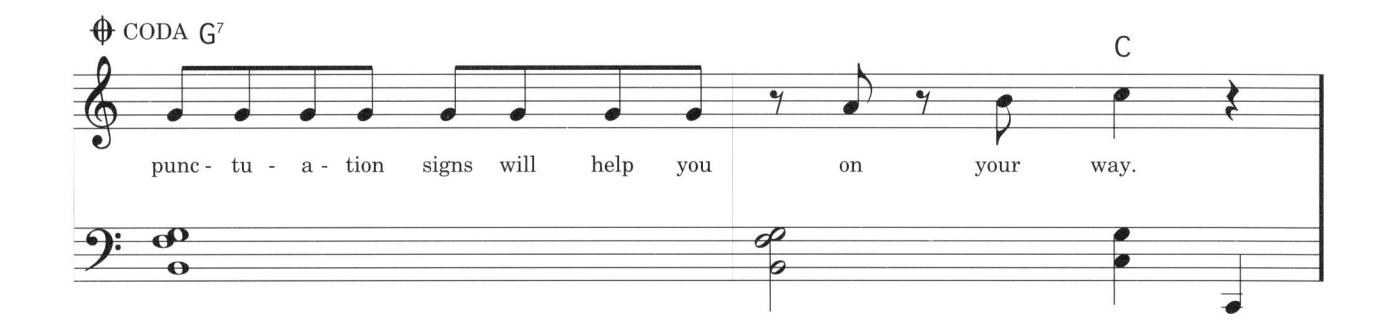

PUNCTUATION SIGNS

[Music notation: Coda section with lyrics "punc-tu-a-tion signs will help you on your way."]

Chorus
As you journey through each sentence,
Signs will help you on your way.
As you journey through each sentence,
Punctuation signs will help you on
   your way.

1.
Watch out for the smallest sign,
Its special message send
When you've written down a sentence,
Put a full stop at the end.

Chorus

2.
If you write a question, like
'Are you coming to the park?'
Then the sign you need at sentence end
Is just a question mark.

Chorus

3.
When you write a warning
Such as 'Look out!', 'Mind the Shark!',
And for anger or surprise,
You need an exclamation mark.

Chorus

4.
Put inverted commas
Round the words that people say.
As you journey through the sentence,
They will help you on your way.

Chorus

5.
A comma in a sentence
Means a pause is needed here.
As you journey through the sentence,
It will make the meaning clear.

As you journey through each sentence,
Signs will help you on your way.
As you journey through each sentence,
Punctuation signs will help you on
   your way.
Punctuation signs will help you on
   your way.

Punctuation Signs

Chorus
As you journey through each sentence,
Signs will help you on your way.
As you journey through each sentence,
Punctuation signs will help you on your way.

1. Watch out for the smallest sign,
   Its special message send
   When you've written down a sentence,
   Put a full stop at the end.

Chorus

2. If you write a question, like
   'Are you coming to the park?'
   Then the sign you need at sentence end
   Is just a question mark.

Chorus

3. When you write a warning
   Such as 'Look out!', 'Mind the Shark!',
   And for anger or surprise,
   You need an exclamation mark.

Chorus

4. Put inverted commas
   Round the words that people say.
   As you journey through the sentence,
   They will help you on your way.

Chorus

5. A comma in a sentence
   Means a pause is needed here.
   As you journey through the sentence,
   It will make the meaning clear.

As you journey through each sentence,
Signs will help you on your way.
As you journey through each sentence,
Punctuation signs will help you on your way.
Punctuation signs will help you on your way.

The Writing's on the Wall

Peter Morrell

1. Ev'ry Friday afternoon I take my homework home. Sometimes it's a story, or some maths, or write a poem. This week's task I'll have to ask someone who's in the know, 'cos I've to write in a certain style, let my imagination flow. Oh no, oh woe, please show me how.

WRITING

THE WRITING'S ON THE WALL

let's make hay, no time to waste. For the writing's on the wall, there are shelves with books galore. There's a paper on the table, there are comics on your bedroom floor.

(Spoken) Tidy 'em up! You're surrounded by a range of writing all you have to do is paint a vivid picture with the words that you choose. words that you choose.

© pfp publishing ltd 1998 • ISBN 1 874050 41 4
May be photocopied for use only within the purchasing institution
pfp 61 Gray's Inn Road London WC1X 8TL

61

1.
Ev'ry Friday afternoon I take my homework home.
Sometimes it's a story, or some maths or write a poem.
This week's task I'll have to ask someone who's in the know
'Cos I've to write in a certain style, let my imagination flow.
Oh no, oh woe, please show me how.

2.
Look at all the different kinds of writing you can find,
Sports reports and book reviews, there's plays of many kinds.
Novel, stories, thrillers, don't forget 'Who's done it?' tales,
By authors living in times gone by as well as writers here today.
So let's make hay, no time to waste.

Chorus
For the writing's on the wall, there are shelves with books galore.
There's a paper on the table, there are comics on your bedroom floor.
   (Spoken) Tidy 'em up!
You're surrounded by a range of writing all you have to do
Is paint a vivid picture with the words that you choose.

3.
Once you have decided what you want to write about,
'Go for it!' and finish it and then you can chill out.
Writing for an audience can bring its own reward.
As someone wrote in the mists of time, 'The pen is mightier than the sword'.
So open the door and look around.

Chorus

The Writing's on the Wall

1.
Ev'ry Friday afternoon I take my homework home.
Sometimes it's a story, or some maths or write a poem.
This week's task I'll have to ask someone who's in the know
'Cos I've to write in a certain style, let my imagination flow.
Oh no, oh woe, please show me how.

2.
Look at all the different kinds of writing you can find,
Sports reports and book reviews, there's plays of many kinds.
Novel, stories, thrillers, don't forget 'Who's done it?' tales,
By authors living in times gone by as well as writers here today.
So let's make hay, no time to waste.

Chorus
For the writing's on the wall, there are shelves with books galore.
There's a paper on the table, there are comics on your bedroom floor.
   (Spoken) Tidy 'em up!
You're surrounded by a range of writing all you have to do
Is paint a vivid picture with the words that you choose.

3.
Once you have decided what you want to write about,
'Go for it!' and finish it and then you can chill out.
Writing for an audience can bring its own reward.
As someone wrote in the mists of time, 'The pen is mightier than
   the sword'.
So open the door and look around.

Chorus

Similes

Clive Barnwell

Mighty as a wave.
Silent as a star.
Deep as velvet seas.
Green as summer trees.
Violent as a storm.
Ancient as the hills.
Gentle as a breeze.
These are similes.

Chorus
Powerful as kings. Bright as diamond rings. Free as birds that soar on their open wings.
Soft as seaside sand. Firm as solid land. Loud as standing next to a marching band.
Ev'rybody sees diff'rently and
Ev'rybody sees diff'rently and

WRITING — SIMILES

1.
Mighty as a wave.
Deep as velvet seas.
Violent as a storm.
Gentle as a breeze.
Silent as a star.
Green as summer trees.
Ancient as the hills.
These are similes.

Chorus
Powerful as kings.
Bright as diamond rings.
Free as birds that soar
On their open wings.
Everybody sees
Differently and these
Make up similes.
Soft as seaside sand.
Firm as solid land.
Loud as standing next to
A marching band.
Everybody sees
Differently and these
Make up similes.

2.
Fragile as a flower.
Golden as a dawn.
Gentle as a cloud.
Pointed as a thorn.
Bigger than a world.
Greater still than these.
The power of the word
Creating similes.

Chorus

Similes

1.
Mighty as a wave.
Deep as velvet seas.
Violent as a storm.
Gentle as a breeze.
Silent as a star.
Green as summer trees.
Ancient as the hills.
These are similes.

Chorus
Powerful as kings.
Bright as diamond rings.
Free as birds that soar
On their open wings.
Everybody sees
Differently and these
Make up similes.
Soft as seaside sand.
Firm as solid land.
Loud as standing next to
A marching band.
Everybody sees
Differently and these
Make up similes.

2.
Fragile as a flower.
Golden as a dawn.
Gentle as a cloud.
Pointed as a thorn.
Bigger than a world.
Greater still than these.
The power of the word
Creating similes.

Chorus

Capital Letter Blues

Peter Morrell

Sadly

Oh dum de doo I've got the ca-pi-tal let-ter blues.

Oh dum de doe I real-ly don't know where they go.

Oh dum de dee oh won't you please, please help me.

Brightly Now lis-ten ve-ry care-ful-ly we'll try to help you out. Here's where those cap-i-tal let-ters go so

CAPITAL LETTER BLUES — WRITING

you are in no doubt. 1. There's count-ries, count-ies, ci-ties, towns, Lap-land, Lon-don and Coun-ty Down. Hog-ma-nay. Christ-mas Day. And... 5. Streets and squares and lanes and roads, Ram-say, Al-bert and By-ker Grove. B B C. I T V. And... 9. Week-days, months, names, sea-sons all, Tues-day, Ap-ril and Spring and Fall. dish from Sky.

68

© pfp publishing ltd 1998 • ISBN 1 874050 41 4
May be photocopied for use only within the purchasing institution
pfp 61 Gray's Inn Road London WC1X 8TL

WRITING — CAPITAL LETTER BLUES

What a price! And... 13. Famous planes and trains and ships, Spitfire, Rocket and Titanic. in a flap. So... 17. If you follow all our clues, no more suff'ring from the capital letter blues. Bye, bye the blues!

CAPITAL LETTER BLUES

Oh dum de doo
I've got the capital letter blues.
Oh dum de doe
I really don't know where they go.
Oh dum de dee
Oh won't you please, please help me.

Now listen very carefully,
We'll try and help you out.
Here's where those capital letters go
So you are in no doubt.

1.
There's countries, counties, cities, towns,
Lapland, London and County Down.

2.
Mountains, hills and people's names,
Everest, Snowdon, Tarzan, Jane.

3.
Oceans, rivers, lakes and seas,
Indian, Amazon, Zueider Zee.

4.
Special places, special days,
Alton Towers and Hogmanay.
Christmas Day. And…

5.
Streets and squares and lanes and roads,
Ramsey, Albert and Byker Grove.

6.
Titles go in front of names,
Doctor, Sir and Queen of Spain.

7.
Pop stars, film stars, stars up high,
Spice Girls, Popeye and Gemini.

8.
Abbreviations like BFG,
M&S, SOS and BBC.
ITV. And…

9.
Weekdays, month names, seasons all,
Tuesday, April and Spring and Fall.

10.
Sports teams, ice creams, coffee, tea,
Spurs, Fab, Kenco and Brooke Bond D.

11.
TV programmes, books and films,
Neighbours, The Bible and Gone with
   the Wind.

12.
Firms with things for us to buy,
Woolies, Microsoft, dish from Sky.
What a price! And…

13.
Famous planes and trains and ships,
Spitfire, Rocket and Titanic.

14.
Planets, papers, proper nouns,
Pluto, Funday Times, Watership Down.

15.
Theatres, schools, when will it stop?
Globe, St. Trinian's, Body Shop.

16.
Start a sentence with a CAP*,
Then you won't get in a flap.
So…

17.
If you follow all our clues
No more suff'ring from the capital letter
   blues.
Bye, bye the blues!

*capital letter

Capital Letter Blues

Oh dum de doo
I've got the capital letter blues.
Oh dum de doe
I really don't know where they go.
Oh dum de dee
Oh won't you please, please
   help me.

Now listen very carefully,
We'll try and help you out.
Here's where those capital
   letters go
So you are in no doubt.

1.
There's countries, counties, cities,
   towns,
Lapland, London and County
   Down.

2.
Mountains, hills and people's
   names,
Everest, Snowdon, Tarzan, Jane.

3.
Oceans, rivers, lakes and seas,
Indian, Amazon, Zueider Zee.

4.
Special places, special days,
Alton Towers and Hogmanay.
Christmas Day. And...

5.
Streets and squares and lanes
   and roads,
Ramsey, Albert and Byker Grove.

6.
Titles go in front of names,
Doctor, Sir and Queen of Spain.

7.
Pop stars, film stars, stars up
   high,
Spice Girls, Popeye and Gemini.

8.
Abbreviations like BFG.
M&S, SOS and BBC.
ITV. And...

9.
Weekdays, month names,
   seasons all,
Tuesday, April and Spring and Fall.

Capital Letter Blues (continued)

10.
Sports teams, ice creams, coffee, tea,
Spurs, Fab, Kenco and Brooke Bond D.

11.
TV programmes, books and films,
Neighbours, The Bible and Gone with the Wind.

12.
Firms with things for us to buy,
Woolies, Microsoft, dish from Sky.
What a price! And...

13.
Famous planes and trains and ships,
Spitfire, Rocket and Titanic.

14.
Planets, papers, proper nouns,
Pluto, Funday Times, Watership Down.

15.
Theatres, schools, when will it stop?
Globe, St. Trinian's, Body Shop.

16.
Start a sentence with a CAP*,
Then you won't get in a flap.
So...

17.
If you follow all our clues
No more suff'ring from the capital letter blues.
Bye, bye the blues!

*capital letter

ADDITION   *DINOSAURS*

Dinosaurs

Susan Eames

Chorus: Di-no-saurs are com-ing, Di-no-saurs are com-ing.
Clomp, clomp-et-ty clomp. Clomp, clomp-et-ty clomp.

Verse: 1. One and one, that makes two. Di-no-saurs are com-ing to you.

DINOSAURS — ADDITION

Chorus
Dinosaurs are coming!
Dinosaurs are coming!
Clomp, clompetty clomp.
Clomp clompetty clomp.

1.
One and one, that makes two.
Dinosaurs are coming to you.

Chorus

2.
Two and two, that makes four.
Dinosaurs are coming once more.

Chorus

3.
Three and three, that makes six.
Dinosaurs are up to their tricks.

Chorus

4.
Four and four, that makes eight.
Dinosaurs are never late.

Chorus

5.
Five and five, that makes ten.
Dinosaurs are going again.

Chorus
Dinosaurs are going!
Dinosaurs are going!
Clomp, clompetty clomp.
Clomp clompetty clomp.

Dinosaurs

Chorus
Dinosaurs are coming!
Dinosaurs are coming!
Clomp, clompetty clomp.
Clomp clompetty clomp.

1.
One and one, that makes two.
Dinosaurs are coming to you.

Chorus

2.
Two and two, that makes four.
Dinosaurs are coming once more.

Chorus

3.
Three and three, that makes six.
Dinosaurs are up to their tricks.

Chorus

4.
Four and four, that makes eight.
Dinosaurs are never late.

Chorus

5.
Five and five, that makes ten.
Dinosaurs are going again.

Chorus
Dinosaurs are going!
Dinosaurs are going!
Clomp, clompetty clomp.
Clomp clompetty clomp.

Ten Fat Caterpillars

Susan Eames

Ten fat caterpillars crawling in the garden.
Ten fat caterpillars crawling on a leaf.
Ten fat caterpillars crawling on a cabbage leaf.
Ten on top. How many underneath? None!

ADDITION

TEN FAT CATERPILLARS

Ten fat caterpillars crawling in the garden,
Ten fat caterpillars crawling on a leaf,
Ten fat caterpillars crawling on a cabbage leaf.
Ten on top. How many underneath?
None!

Ten fat caterpillars crawling in the garden,
Ten fat caterpillars crawling on a leaf,
Ten fat caterpillars crawling on a cabbage leaf.
Nine on top. How many underneath?
One!

Ten fat caterpillars crawling in the garden,
Ten fat caterpillars crawling on a leaf,
Ten fat caterpillars crawling on a cabbage leaf.
Eight on top. How many underneath?
Two!

Ten fat caterpillars crawling in the garden,
Ten fat caterpillars crawling on a leaf,
Ten fat caterpillars crawling on a cabbage leaf.
Seven on top. How many underneath?
Three!

Ten fat caterpillars crawling in the garden,
Ten fat caterpillars crawling on a leaf,
Ten fat caterpillars crawling on a cabbage leaf.
Six on top. How many underneath?
Four!

Ten fat caterpillars crawling in the garden,
Ten fat caterpillars crawling on a leaf,
Ten fat caterpillars crawling on a cabbage leaf.
Five on top. How many underneath?
Five!

Ten fat caterpillars crawling in the garden,
Ten fat caterpillars crawling on a leaf,
Ten fat caterpillars crawling on a cabbage leaf.
Four on top. How many underneath?
Six!

Ten fat caterpillars crawling in the garden,
Ten fat caterpillars crawling on a leaf,
Ten fat caterpillars crawling on a cabbage leaf.
Three on top. How many underneath?
Seven!

Ten fat caterpillars crawling in the garden,
Ten fat caterpillars crawling on a leaf,
Ten fat caterpillars crawling on a cabbage leaf.
Two on top. How many underneath?
Eight!

Ten fat caterpillars crawling in the garden,
Ten fat caterpillars crawling on a leaf,
Ten fat caterpillars crawling on a cabbage leaf.
One on top. How many underneath?
Nine!

Ten fat caterpillars crawling in the garden,
Ten fat caterpillars crawling on a leaf,
Ten fat caterpillars crawling on a cabbage leaf.
None on top. How many underneath?
Ten!

Ten Fat Caterpillars

Ten fat caterpillars crawling in the garden,
Ten fat caterpillars crawling on a leaf,
Ten fat caterpillars crawling on a cabbage leaf.
Ten on top. How many underneath?
None!

Ten fat caterpillars crawling in the garden,
Ten fat caterpillars crawling on a leaf,
Ten fat caterpillars crawling on a cabbage leaf.
Nine on top. How many underneath?
One!

Ten fat caterpillars crawling in the garden,
Ten fat caterpillars crawling on a leaf,
Ten fat caterpillars crawling on a cabbage leaf.
Eight on top. How many underneath?
Two!

Ten fat caterpillars crawling in the garden,
Ten fat caterpillars crawling on a leaf,
Ten fat caterpillars crawling on a cabbage leaf.
Seven on top. How many underneath?
Three!

Ten fat caterpillars crawling in the garden,
Ten fat caterpillars crawling on a leaf,
Ten fat caterpillars crawling on a cabbage leaf.
Six on top. How many underneath?
Four!

Ten fat caterpillars crawling in the garden,
Ten fat caterpillars crawling on a leaf,
Ten fat caterpillars crawling on a cabbage leaf.
Five on top. How many underneath?
Five!

Ten fat caterpillars crawling in the garden,
Ten fat caterpillars crawling on a leaf,
Ten fat caterpillars crawling on a cabbage leaf.
Four on top. How many underneath?
Six!

Ten fat caterpillars crawling in the garden,
Ten fat caterpillars crawling on a leaf,
Ten fat caterpillars crawling on a cabbage leaf.
Three on top. How many underneath?
Seven!

Ten fat caterpillars crawling in the garden,
Ten fat caterpillars crawling on a leaf,
Ten fat caterpillars crawling on a cabbage leaf.
Two on top. How many underneath?
Eight!

Ten fat caterpillars crawling in the garden,
Ten fat caterpillars crawling on a leaf,
Ten fat caterpillars crawling on a cabbage leaf.
One on top. How many underneath?
Nine!

Ten fat caterpillars crawling in the garden,
Ten fat caterpillars crawling on a leaf,
Ten fat caterpillars crawling on a cabbage leaf.
None on top. How many underneath?
Ten!

Cutting Corners

Maurice Walsh

A right-angled triangle isn't very hard to wangle, you can do it if you're eight or eighty two. You need scissors for this caper and a piece of A5 paper, now listen while I tell you what to do. Do not try this in the sauna (soggy paper), snip the corner of the page with the scissors; hold it there, right there. Your tri-

CUTTING CORNERS

[Musical notation with lyrics:]

an-gle (well, well, well!) will have one an-gle like an 'L': that's the right an-gle, the cor-ner of a square. That's a nine-ty de-gree right an-gle you have there!

1.
A right-angled triangle
Isn't very hard to wangle,
You can do it if you're eight or eighty-two.
You need scissors for this caper
And a piece of A5 paper,
Now listen while I tell you what to do.
Do not try this in the sauna (soggy paper),
Snip the corner of the page with the scissors;
Hold it there, right there,
Your triangle (well, well, well!) will have one angle like an 'L':
That's the right angle, the corner of a square.
That's a ninety-degree right angle you have there!

2.
If you want to disentangle
Diff'rent versions of triangle,
You will need to learn their names right now, this week.
Equilateral's a word
That is Latin – so I've heard,
While Isosceles and Scalene both are Greek.
If all three sides are the same,
Then Equilateral is the name;
If it's only two, Isosceles it is, it is.
While if none of the sides is equal,
Each one different, all unequal,
It's a Scalene triangle and you're a whiz!
It's a Scalene triangle; you've done the biz!

Cutting Corners

1.
A right-angled triangle
Isn't very hard to wangle,
You can do it if you're eight or eighty-two.
You need scissors for this caper
And a piece of A5 paper,
Now listen while I tell you what to do.
Do not try this in the sauna (soggy paper),
Snip the corner of the page with the scissors;
Hold it there, right there,
Your triangle (well, well, well!) will have one angle like
   an 'L':
That's the right angle, the corner of a square.
That's a ninety-degree right angle you have there!

2.
If you want to disentangle
Diff'rent versions of triangle,
You will need to learn their names right now, this week.
Equilateral's a word
That is Latin – so I've heard,
While Isosceles and Scalene both are Greek.
If all three sides are the same,
Then Equilateral is the name;
If it's only two, Isosceles it is, it is.
While if none of the sides is equal,
Each one different, all unequal,
It's a Scalene triangle and you're a whiz!
It's a Scalene triangle; you've done the biz!

One Knock at the Door

Johanne Levy

COUNTING — ONE KNOCK AT THE DOOR

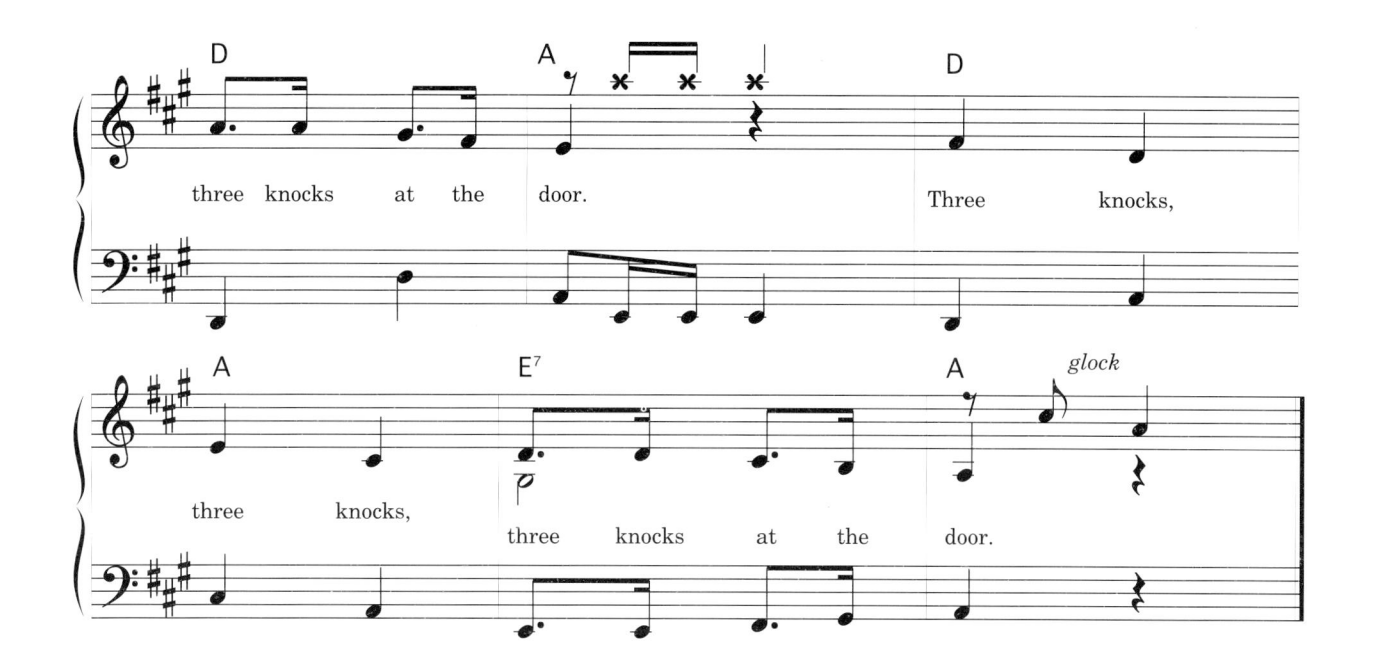

1.
There was one knock at the door,
One knock at the door.
One knock, one knock,
One knock at the door.

2.
There were two knocks at the door,
Two knocks at the door.
Two knocks, two knocks,
Two knocks at the door.

3.
There were three knocks at the door,
Three knocks at the door.
Three knocks, three knocks,
Three knocks at the door.

One Knock at the Door

1.
There was one knock at the door,
One knock at the door.
One knock, one knock,
One knock at the door.

2.
There were two knocks at the door,
Two knocks at the door.
Two knocks, two knocks,
Two knocks at the door.

3.
There were three knocks at the door,
Three knocks at the door.
Three knocks, three knocks,
Three knocks at the door.

Cornucopia

Jean Gilbert

We'll have ten grape clusters, purple, black and green. Nine juicy plums all with a purple sheen. Eight velvet peaches glowing pink and gold, and seven rosy apples, crisp and cool to hold. We'll have six bunched bananas, gently curving round. Five perfumed pears, the best that can be found. Four tangerines, so tangy and so sweet.

We'll have ten grape clusters, purple, black and green.
Nine juicy plums all with a purple sheen.
Eight velvet peaches glowing pink and gold,
And seven rosy apples, crisp and cool to hold.
We'll have six bunched bananas, gently curving round.
Five perfumed pears, the best that can be found.
Four tangerines, so tangy and so sweet.
Three pink mangoes, what a lovely treat!
Two ripe melons, freshly cut to eat,
And one pineapple, making it complete.

Cornucopia

We'll have ten grape clusters, purple, black and green.
Nine juicy plums all with a purple sheen.
Eight velvet peaches glowing pink and gold,
And seven rosy apples, crisp and cool to hold.
We'll have six bunched bananas, gently curving round.
Five perfumed pears, the best that can be found.
Four tangerines, so tangy and so sweet.
Three pink mangoes, what a lovely treat!
Two ripe melons, freshly cut to eat,
And one pineapple, making it complete.

Count Your Fingers

Johanne Levy

1.
Leader:
1 2 3 4.

Echo:
1 2 3 4.

Leader:
Sit on the floor.

Echo:
Sit on the floor.

Leader:
Count your fingers.

Echo:
Count your fingers.

All:
1 2 3 4 5 6 7 8 9 and 10.

2.
Leader:
1 2 3 4.

Echo:
1 2 3 4.

Leader:
We'll do some more.

Echo:
We'll do some more.

Leader:
Count your fingers.

Echo:
Count your fingers.

All:
1 2 3 4 5 6 7 8 9 and 10.

Count Your Fingers

1.
1 2 3 4.
1 2 3 4.
Sit on the floor.
Sit on the floor.
Count your fingers.
Count your fingers.
1 2 3 4 5 6 7 8 9 and 10.

2.
1 2 3 4.
1 2 3 4.
We'll do some more.
We'll do some more.
Count your fingers.
Count your fingers.
1 2 3 4 5 6 7 8 9 and 10.

Sausage Boogie

Gerald Haigh

Six - ty one su - per - fine suc - cu - lent sau - sa - ges

sizz - ling on my bar - be - cue.

Six - ty one su - per - fine suc - cu - lent sau - sa - ges

sizz - ling on my bar - be - cue.

Ev' - ry bo - dy wants some, ev' - ry - one will get some.

DIVISION

SAUSAGE BOOGIE

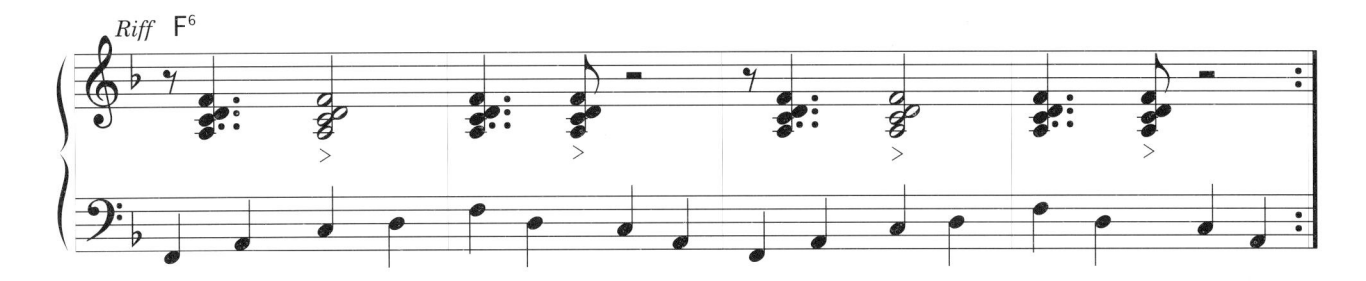

1.
Sixty-one superfine succulent sausages sizzling on my barbecue.
Sixty-one superfine succulent sausages sizzling on my barbecue.
Everybody wants some, everyone will get some.
Get into a tidy queue.

2.
You all want some succulent sausages sizzling on my barbecue.
Come and get some succulent sausages sizzling on my barbecue.
Fifteen people want some, fifteen folk will get some.
If you form a tidy queue.

3.
Margie, Argie, Shulie, Julie, Renata, Ron and Sue.
Jimbo, Bimbo, Jonty, Monty, Gordon, Glen and Boo.
Auntie Philomena. Has anybody seen her?
Tell her what she has to do.

4.
Margie here are four, Argie here are four, Shulie here are four for you.
Julie here are four, Renata here are four, Ron another four for you.
Sue bring your plate – you won't have to wait!
Four is what your share is too.

5.
Jimbo here are four, Bimbo here are four, Jonty here are four for you.
Monty here are four, Gordon here are four, Glen another four for you.
Boo bring your plate – you won't have to wait.
Four is what your share is too.

(Spoken) Anyone left out – Auntie Philomena?

6.
Everyone has four, nobody has more. Sixty-one between fifteen.
Everyone has four, nobody has more. The fairest share I've ever seen.
Auntie Philomena, anybody seen her?
Four for you, we can't be mean.

(Spoken) How many sausages gone? Sixty.
How many left? One.
That's mine!
Sixty-one divided by fifteen. Answer, four remainder one.

Sausage Boogie

1.
Sixty-one superfine succulent sausages sizzling on my barbecue.
Sixty-one superfine succulent sausages sizzling on my barbecue.
Everybody wants some, everyone will get some.
Get into a tidy queue.

2.
You all want some succulent sausages sizzling on my barbecue.
Come and get some succulent sausages sizzling on my barbecue.
Fifteen people want some, fifteen folk will get some.
If you form a tidy queue.

3.
Margie, Argie, Shulie, Julie, Renata, Ron and Sue.
Jimbo, Bimbo, Jonty, Monty, Gordon, Glen and Boo.
Auntie Philomena. Has anybody seen her?
Tell her what she has to do.

4.
Margie here are four, Argie here are four, Shulie here are four for you.
Julie here are four, Renata here are four, Ron another four for you.
Sue bring your plate – you won't have to wait!
Four is what your share is too.

Sausage Boogie (continued)

5.
Jimbo here are four, Bimbo here are four, Jonty here are four for you.
Monty here are four, Gordon here are four, Glen another four for you.
Boo bring your plate – you won't have to wait.
Four is what your share is too.

(Spoken) Anyone left out – Auntie Philomena?

6.
Everyone has four, nobody has more. Sixty-one between fifteen.
Everyone has four, nobody has more. The fairest share I've ever seen.
Auntie Philomena, anybody seen her?
Four for you, we can't be mean.

(Spoken) How many sausages gone? Sixty.
How many left? One.
That's mine!
Sixty-one divided by fifteen. Answer, four remainder one.

Sharing

Susan Eames

Twenty coloured pencils
On the table,
Twenty coloured pencils
Ready to share.
Put them into two pots,
Share them out evenly.
Look at one pot.
How many there?

Ten!

Sharing

Twenty coloured pencils
On the table,
Twenty coloured pencils
Ready to share.
Put them into two pots.
Share them out evenly.
Look at one pot.
How many there?

Ten!

Twenty-Four Pieces – Wow!

Maurice Walsh

1. My Gran gave me a big bar of cho-co-late: twen-ty four pie-ces WOW! Now I'm a cho-co-ho-lic so I shared it with my-self, I had twen-ty four pie-ces WOW!

(spoken) 24 shared by one is 24 *(sung)* 2. Then

DIVISION — TWENTY-FOUR PIECES – WOW!

1.
My Gran gave me a big bar of chocolate:
Twenty-four pieces – WOW!
Now I'm a chocoholic so I shared it with myself,
I had twenty-four pieces – WOW!
(Spoken) 24 shared by 1 is 24.

2.
Then up comes Lee (now Lee LOVES chocolate):
Twenty-four pieces – WOW!
That's two chocoholics, twenty-four pieces,
How many pieces each now?
(Spoken) 24 shared by 2 is 12.

3.
Then up comes Leeanne (now Leeanne LOVES chocolate):
Twenty-four pieces – WOW!
That's three chocoholics, twenty-four pieces,
How many pieces each now?
(Spoken) 24 shared by 3 is 8.

4.
Then up comes Liam (now Liam LOVES chocolate):
Twenty-four pieces – WOW!
That's four chocoholics, twenty-four pieces,
How many pieces each now?
(Spoken) 24 shared by 4 is 6.

5.
Then up comes Leah (now Leah LOVES chocolate):
Twenty-four pieces – WOW!
That's five chocoholics, twenty-four pieces,
How many pieces each now?
(Spoken) 24 shared by 5 is 4 and 4 pieces left over for me!

6.
Then up comes Leroy (now Leroy LOVES chocolate):
Twenty-four pieces – WOW!
That's six chocoholics, twenty-four pieces,
How many pieces each now?
(Spoken) 24 shared by 6 is 4.

7.
Then up comes Lou (now Lou LOVES chocolate):
Twenty-four pieces – WOW!
That's seven chocoholics, twenty-four pieces,
How many pieces each now?
(Spoken) 24 shared by 7 is 3 and 3 pieces left over for me!

8.
Then up comes Lol (now Lol LOVES chocolate):
Twenty-four pieces – WOW!
That's eight chocoholics, twenty-four pieces,
How many pieces each now?
(Spoken) 24 shared by 8 is 3.

9.
Then up comes Lara (now Lara LOVES chocolate):
Twenty-four pieces – WOW!
That's nine chocoholics, twenty-four pieces,
How many pieces each now?
(Spoken) 24 shared by 9 is 2 and 6 pieces left over for me!

10.
Then up comes Lennox (now Lennox LOVES chocolate):
Twenty-four pieces – WOW!
That's ten chocoholics, twenty-four pieces,
How many pieces each now?
(Spoken) 24 shared by 10 is 2 and 4 pieces left over for me!

11.
Then up comes Lil (now Lil LOVES chocolate):
Twenty-four pieces – WOW!
That's eleven chocoholics, twenty-four pieces,
How many pieces each now?
(Spoken) 24 shared by 11 is 2 and 2 pieces left over for me!

12.
Then up comes Lottie (now Lottie LOVES chocolate):
Twenty-four pieces – WOW!
That's twelve chocoholics, twenty-four pieces,
How many pieces each now?
(Spoken) 24 shared by 12 is 2.

THE LITERACY AND NUMERACY SONG BOOK

Twenty-Four Pieces — Wow!

1. My Gran gave me a big bar of chocolate:
   Twenty-four pieces — WOW!
   Now I'm a chocoholic so I shared it with myself,
   I had twenty-four pieces — WOW!
   (Spoken) 24 shared by 1 is 24.

2. Then up comes Lee (now Lee LOVES chocolate):
   Twenty-four pieces — WOW!
   That's two chocoholics, twenty-four pieces,
   How many pieces each now?
   (Spoken) 24 shared by 2 is 12.

3. Then up comes Leeanne (now Leeanne LOVES chocolate):
   Twenty-four pieces — WOW!
   That's three chocoholics, twenty-four pieces,
   How many pieces each now?
   (Spoken) 24 shared by 3 is 8.

4. Then up comes Liam (now Liam LOVES chocolate):
   Twenty-four pieces — WOW!
   That's four chocoholics, twenty-four pieces,
   How many pieces each now?
   (Spoken) 24 shared by 4 is 6.

5. Then up comes Leah (now Leah LOVES chocolate):
   Twenty-four pieces — WOW!
   That's five chocoholics, twenty-four pieces,
   How many pieces each now?
   (Spoken) 24 shared by 5 is 4 and 4 pieces left over for me!

6. Then up comes Leroy (now Leroy LOVES chocolate):
   Twenty-four pieces — WOW!
   That's six chocoholics, twenty-four pieces,
   How many pieces each now?
   (Spoken) 24 shared by 6 is 4.

© pfp publishing ltd 1998 • ISBN 1 874050 41 4
May be photocopied for use only within the purchasing institution
pfp 61 Gray's Inn Road London WC1X 8TL

Twenty-Four Pieces – Wow! (continued)

7. Then up comes Lou (now Lou LOVES chocolate):
   Twenty-four pieces – WOW!
   That's seven chocoholics, twenty-four pieces,
   How many pieces each now?
   (Spoken) 24 shared by 7 is 3 and 3 pieces left over for me!

8. Then up comes Lol (now Lol LOVES chocolate):
   Twenty-four pieces – WOW!
   That's eight chocoholics, twenty-four pieces,
   How many pieces each now?
   (Spoken) 24 shared by 8 is 3.

9. Then up comes Lara (now Lara LOVES chocolate):
   Twenty-four pieces – WOW!
   That's nine chocoholics, twenty-four pieces,
   How many pieces each now?
   (Spoken) 24 shared by 9 is 2 and 6 pieces left over for me!

10. Then up comes Lennox (now Lennox LOVES chocolate):
    Twenty-four pieces – WOW!
    That's ten chocoholics, twenty-four pieces,
    How many pieces each now?
    (Spoken) 24 shared by 10 is 2 and 4 pieces left over for me!

11. Then up comes Lil (now Lil LOVES chocolate):
    Twenty-four pieces – WOW!
    That's eleven chocoholics, twenty-four pieces,
    How many pieces each now?
    (Spoken) 24 shared by 11 is 2 and 2 pieces left over for me!

12. Then up comes Lottie (now Lottie LOVES chocolate):
    Twenty-four pieces – WOW!
    That's twelve chocoholics, twenty-four pieces,
    How many pieces each now?
    (Spoken) 24 shared by 12 is 2.

Peter Metre Eater

Daivid Moses

1. Peter is a metre eater. He can step a whole metre.
2. Rita's step is so much neater. Her step measures half a metre.
4. If they walk for twenty metres think how tired poor Rita's feet are.

(1st ending) Stretch and step a whole metre, all in one stride.

(2 & 3) Half the step of Peter, walking side by side. It's OK for Peter, his stride is wide. 3. When

Pete and Rita walk along together, what do you think they're going to do?

MEASUREMENT

PETER METRE EATER

1.
Peter is a metre eater.
He can step a whole metre.
Stretch and step a whole metre,
All in one stride.

2.
Rita's step is so much neater.
Her step measures half a metre.
Half the step of Peter, walking
Side by side.

3.
When Pete and Rita walk along together,
What do you think they're going to do?
For every stretchy big step Peter takes,
Rita's going to need to take two.

4.
If they walk for twenty metres,
Think how tired poor Rita's feet are.
It's OK for Peter,
His stride is wide.

5.
Rita takes two steps,
While Pete takes only one.
If Rita takes a hundred steps,
How far have they gone?

THE LITERACY AND NUMERACY SONG BOOK

Peter Metre Eater

1.
Peter is a metre eater.
He can step a whole metre.
Stretch and step a whole metre,
All in one stride.

2.
Rita's step is so much neater.
Her step measures half a metre.
Half the step of Peter, walking
Side by side.

3.
When Pete and Rita walk along together,
What do you think they're going to do?
For every stretchy big step Peter takes,
Rita's going to need to take two.

4.
If they walk for twenty metres,
Think how tired poor Rita's feet are.
It's OK for Peter,
His stride is wide.

5.
Rita takes two steps,
While Pete takes only one.
If Rita takes a hundred steps,
How far have they gone?

Multiplication March

Maurice Walsh

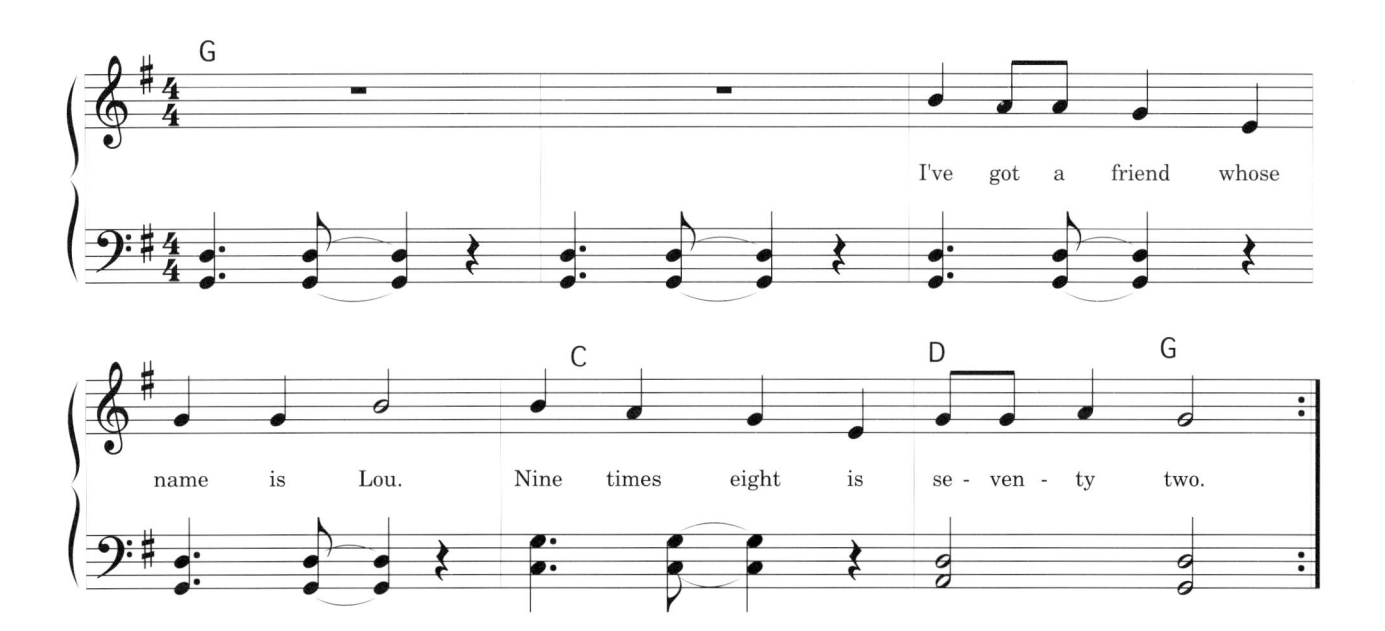

I've got a friend whose name is Lou. Nine times eight is se-ven-ty two.

1.
I've got a friend whose name is Lou.
Nine times eight is seventy-two.

2.
I think Lou is mighty fine.
Seven sevens, forty-nine.

3.
Lou is always at my door.
Six times nine is fifty-four.

4.
I think Lou is keen on me.
Seven nines are sixty-three.

5.
Lou is fun and full of tricks.
Seven eights are fifty-six.

6.
Meeting Lou – I can't be late.
Eight times six is forty-eight.

7.
This song can go on and on.
Eleven elevens are one two one.

Multiplication March

1.
I've got a friend whose name is Lou.
Nine times eight is seventy-two.

2.
I think Lou is mighty fine.
Seven sevens, forty-nine.

3.
Lou is always at my door.
Six times nine is fifty-four.

4.
I think Lou is keen on me.
Seven nines are sixty-three.

5.
Lou is fun and full of tricks.
Seven eights are fifty-six.

6.
Meeting Lou - I can't be late.
Eight times six is forty-eight.

7.
This song can go on and on.
Eleven elevens are one two one.

Soldiers Marching

Susan Eames

SOLDIERS MARCHING

MULTIPLICATION

Soldiers marching, soldiers marching,
Soldiers marching down the street.
Two ones are two, two twos are four.
Soldiers marching past my door.
Two threes are six, two fours are eight.
Soldiers marching past my gate.

Soldiers marching, soldiers marching,
Soldiers marching down the street.
Two ones are two, two twos are four.
Soldiers marching past my door.
Two threes are six, two fours are eight.
Soldiers marching past my gate.

Soldiers Marching

Soldiers marching, soldiers marching,
Soldiers marching down the street.
Two ones are two, two twos are four.
Soldiers marching past my door.
Two threes are six, two fours are eight.
Soldiers marching past my gate.

Soldiers marching, soldiers marching,
Soldiers marching down the street.
Two ones are two, two twos are four.
Soldiers marching past my door.
Two threes are six, two fours are eight.
Soldiers marching past my gate.

The Seven Times Table Song

Maurice Walsh

One se-ven? *Se-ven.* That's an ea-sy start. Two se-vens? *Four-teen.* Soon know this by heart. Three se-vens? *Twen-ty one.* Now you're real-ly groov-in'. Four se-vens? *Twen-ty eight.* I think that you're im-pro-vin'. Hoi!

MULTIPLICATION

THE SEVEN TIMES TABLE SONG

1.
One seven? Seven.
That's an easy start.
Two sevens? Fourteen.
Soon know this by heart.
Three sevens? Twenty-one.
Now you're really groovin'.
Four sevens? Twenty eight.
I think that you're improvin'. Hoi!

2.
Five sevens? Thirty-five.
Well, I do declare!
Six sevens? Forty-two.
Now you're halfway there.
Seven sevens? Forty-nine.
Don't stop, you're doing fine.
Eight sevens? Fifty-six.
Now for number nine. Hoi!

3.
Nine sevens? Sixty-three.
Didn't think you knew it
Ten sevens? Seventy.
Well done, you're nearly through it.
Eleven sevens? Seventy-seven.
One more and you've whacked it.
Twelve sevens? Eighty-four.
YES! You've really cracked it! Hoi!

THE LITERACY AND NUMERACY SONG BOOK

The Seven Times Table Song

1.
One seven? Seven.
That's an easy start.
Two sevens? Fourteen.
Soon know this by heart.
Three sevens? Twenty-one.
Now you're really groovin'.
Four sevens? Twenty eight.
I think that you're improvin'. Hoi!

2.
Five sevens? Thirty-five.
Well, I do declare!
Six sevens? Forty-two.
Now you're halfway there.
Seven sevens? Forty-nine.
Don't stop, you're doing fine.
Eight sevens? Fifty-six.
Now for number nine. Hoi!

3.
Nine sevens? Sixty-three.
Didn't think you knew it
Ten sevens? Seventy.
Well done, you're nearly through it.
Eleven sevens? Seventy-seven.
One more and you've whacked it.
Twelve sevens? Eighty-four.
YES! You've really cracked it! Hoi!

Number Blues

Hazel Hobbs

Steady Swing

I'm one, it's no fun on my own, oh so a-lone. One digit more than none. I'm number one. *(spoken)* I'm number one. (I'm)

1.
I'm one, it's no fun,
On my own, oh so alone.
One digit more, than none.
I'm number one.
(Spoken) I'm number one.

2.
I'm two, but I'm blue,
Just a pair, he's always there,
Ever a couple who
Are number two.
(Spoken) I'm number two.

3.
I'm three, can you see
That I'm odd? Give me a nod.
If you know three's a trio,
Then you know me.
(Spoken) I'm number three.

4.
I'm four, I adore
Being there, sides on a square.
Use me to tap your feet
To a musical beat.
(Spoken) 1, 2, 3, 4.

5.
I'm five, I'm alive.
See your hand, count fingers and
You'll find out then,
I'm half number ten.
(Spoken) I'm number five.

Number Blues

1. I'm one, it's no fun,
   On my own, oh so alone.
   One digit more, than none.
   I'm number one.
   (Spoken) I'm number one.

2. I'm two, but I'm blue,
   Just a pair, he's always there,
   Ever a couple who
   Are number two.
   (Spoken) I'm number two.

3. I'm three, can you see
   That I'm odd? Give me a nod.
   If you know three's a trio,
   Then you know me.
   (Spoken) I'm number three.

4. I'm four, I adore
   Being there, sides on a square.
   Use me to tap your feet
   To a musical beat.
   (Spoken) 1, 2, 3, 4.

5. I'm five, I'm alive.
   See your hand, count fingers and
   You'll find out then,
   I'm half number ten.
   (Spoken) I'm number five.

Day Without Numbers

Hazel Hobbs

1. I-magine a day without numbers. How could we count without numbers? How could we tell the time, eat and get to school by nine? What a problem that would be for you and me.

Fine

2. I-

DAY WITHOUT NUMBERS

1.
Imagine a day without numbers.
How could we count without numbers?
How could we tell the time,
Eat and get to school by nine?
What a problem that would be
For you and me.

2.
Imagine a day without numbers.
How could we count without numbers?
Cook making meals for lunch
Couldn't weigh ingredients.
What a problem that would be
For you and me.

3.
Imagine a day without numbers.
How could we count without numbers?
In games there'd be no fun,
Wouldn't know who scored more runs.
What a problem that would be
For you and me.

4.
Imagine a day without numbers.
How could we count without numbers?
Shelves of books all in a line,
With no numbers on their spines.
What a problem that would be
For you and me.

Day Without Numbers

1. Imagine a day without numbers.
   How could we count without numbers?
   How could we tell the time,
   Eat and get to school by nine?
   What a problem that would be
   For you and me.

2. Imagine a day without numbers.
   How could we count without numbers?
   Cook making meals for lunch
   Couldn't weigh ingredients.
   What a problem that would be
   For you and me.

3. Imagine a day without numbers.
   How could we count without numbers?
   In games there'd be no fun,
   Wouldn't know who scored more runs.
   What a problem that would be
   For you and me.

4. Imagine a day without numbers.
   How could we count without numbers?
   Shelves of books all in a line,
   With no numbers on their spines.
   What a problem that would be
   For you and me.

Clementine

Belinda Morley

Chorus
I'm Clementine the centipede,
I'm very very long,
And as I walk on my hundred feet,
I like to sing this song.

1.
Oh! A snail has only one foot,
A human only two.
But I have got a hundred feet
And fifty pairs of shoes.

Chorus

2.
If I trip or slip or slide
Or one foot goes astray,
I've still got ninety-nine spare feet
To help me on my way.

Chorus

© pfp publishing ltd 1998 • ISBN 1 874050 41 4
May be photocopied for use only within the purchasing institution
pfp 61 Gray's Inn Road London WC1X 8TL

Clementine

Chorus
I'm Clementine the centipede,
I'm very very long,
And as I walk on my hundred feet,
I like to sing this song.

1.
Oh! A snail has only one foot,
A human only two.
But I have got a hundred feet
And fifty pairs of shoes.

Chorus

2.
If I trip or slip or slide
Or one foot goes astray,
I've still got ninety-nine spare feet
To help me on my way.

Chorus

Up, Down, Round About

Maurice Walsh

1. We're going UP the stairs, we're going DOWN the slide. We're looking THROUGH the window at the trees OUT-SIDE. We go A-LONG the street, we go A-ROUND a bend. We sit U-PON the floor, we sit BE-SIDE our friend.

2. You're list-ening WITH your ears, you're list-ening TO a sound. The birds fly O-VER head, the worms live UN-DER ground. You bite BE-TWEEN your teeth, you put your fin-ger ON your lips. You scratch BE-HIND your ear and stick your fork IN-TO your chips.

1.
We're going **up** the stairs,
We're going **down** the slide.
We're looking **through** the window
At the trees **outside**.
We go **along** the street,
We go **around** a bend.
We sit **upon** the floor,
We sit **beside** our friend.

2.
You're listening **with** your ears,
You're listening **to** a sound.
The birds fly **over**head,
The worms live **under**ground.
You bite **between** your teeth,
You put your finger **on** your lips.
You scratch **behind** your ear
And stick your fork **into** your chips.

Up, Down, Round About

1.
We're going <u>up</u> the stairs,
We're going <u>down</u> the slide.
We're looking <u>through</u> the window
At the trees <u>outside</u>.
We go <u>along</u> the street,
We go <u>around</u> a bend.
We sit <u>upon</u> the floor,
We sit <u>beside</u> our friend.

2.
You're listening <u>with</u> your ears,
You're listening <u>to</u> a sound.
The birds fly <u>overhead</u>,
The worms live <u>underground</u>.
You bite <u>between</u> your teeth,
You put your finger <u>on</u> your lips.
You scratch <u>behind</u> your ear
And stick your fork <u>into</u> your chips.

Sir Cumference

Clive Barnwell

1. My name is Sir Cumference, Sir Cull's most trusty knight. Pa-
round and round I go. Never moving off the Sir Cull line. Not straying

2. trolling his border to keep his area right. Far away the centre, y, on the spot and never changing distance, watches

SHAPES

SIR CUMFERENCE

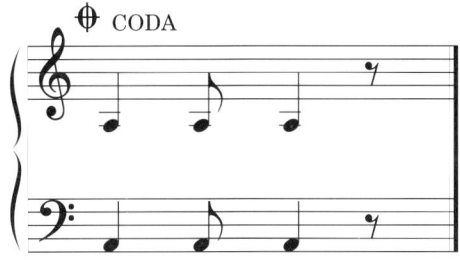

1.
My name is Sir Cumference,
Sir Cull's most trusty knight.
Patrolling his border
To keep his area right.

Round and round and round I go.
Never moving off the Sir Cull line.
Not straying up or down, you know,
In position all the time.

Far away the centrey,
On the spot and never changing
  distance,
Watches very carefully.
I must never go off line.

2.
My name is Di Ameter,
The path I take is straight.
With partner Ray Dius,
We help keep Sir Cull safe.

In a line, so straight we go,
Poor Sir Cumference has to go the long
  way round,
He can't keep up and so
We just leave him far behind.

Helping keep the tangents out,
Making sure the Chords have got a place
  to go.
If we get bigger, we're
Bound to help Sir Cull to grow.

© pfp publishing ltd 1998 • ISBN 1 874050 41 4
May be photocopied for use only within the purchasing institution
pfp 61 Gray's Inn Road London WC1X 8TL

THE LITERACY AND NUMERACY SONG BOOK

Sir Cumference

1.
My name is Sir Cumference,
Sir Cull's most trusty knight.
Patrolling his border
To keep his area right.

Round and round and round I go.
Never moving off the Sir Cull line.
Not straying up or down, you know,
In position all the time.

Far away the centrey,
On the spot and never changing distance,
Watches very carefully.
I must never go off line.

2.
My name is Di Ameter,
The path I take is straight.
With partner Ray Dius,
We help keep Sir Cull safe.

In a line, so straight we go,
Poor Sir Cumference has to go the long way round,
He can't keep up and so
We just leave him far behind.

Helping keep the tangents out,
Making sure the Chords have got a place to go.
If we get bigger, we're
Bound to help Sir Cull to grow.

Symmetry

Maurice Walsh

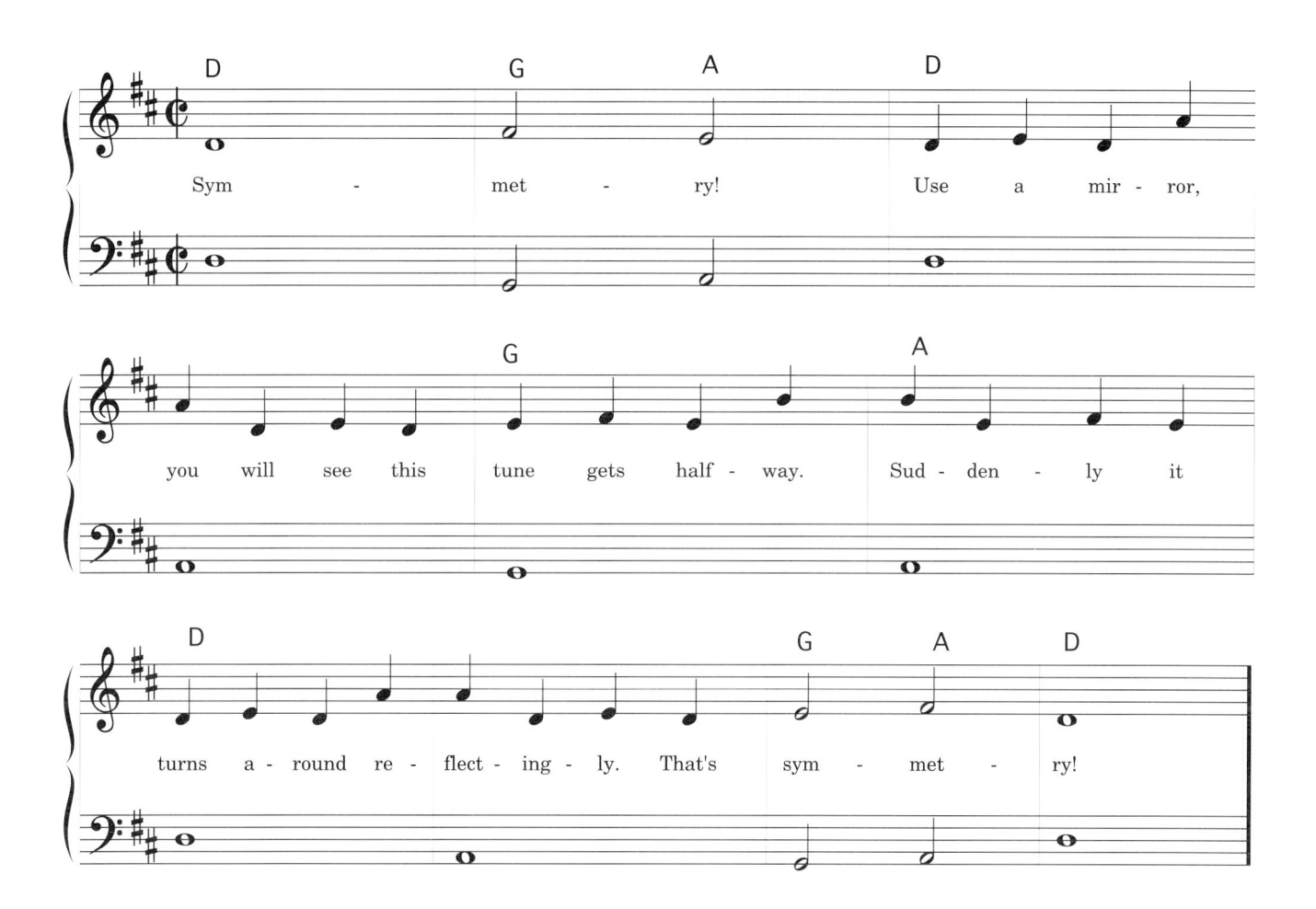

Symmetry! Use a mirror,
You will see this tune gets halfway.
Suddenly it turns around reflectingly.
That's symmetry!

Symmetry

Symmetry! Use a mirror,

You will see this tune gets halfway.

Suddenly it turns around reflectingly.

That's symmetry!

Plane Shapes and Solids

Maurice Walsh

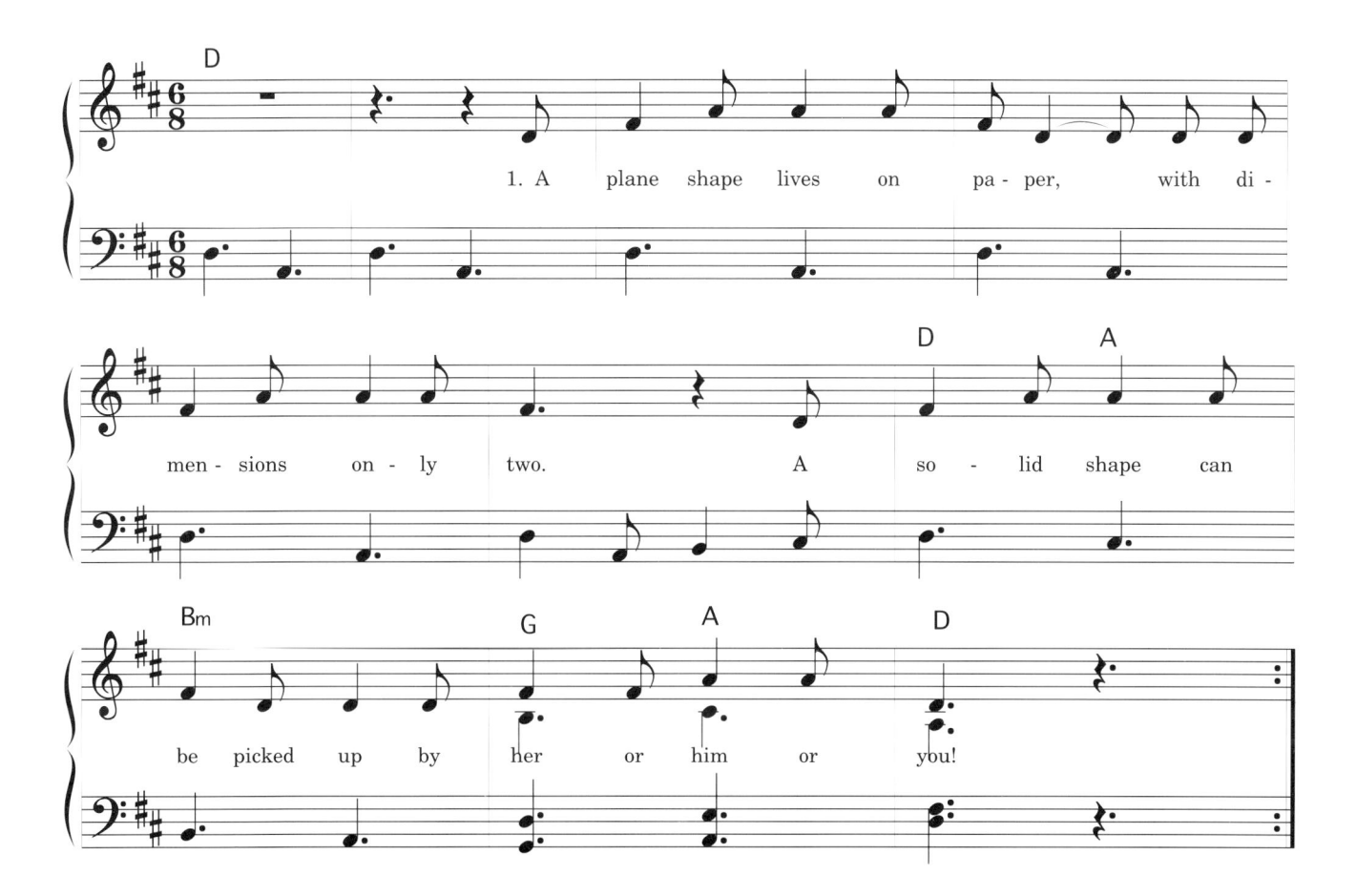

1.
A plane shape lives on paper,
With dimensions only two.
A solid shape can be picked up
By her or him or you!

2.
A plane shape is a drawing
In pencil or in ink.
But a solid you can put things in,
Like an ice-cube in a drink.

3.
A polygon is a plane shape,
With straight sides three, or more.
A triangle has three straight sides,
A rectangle has four.

4.
A house-brick is a cuboid,
A die is a six-faced cube.
A tennis ball is called a sphere,
And a cylinder's a tube.

5.
So now you see the difference:
A solid you can throw.
A plane shape you can only draw,
That's all you need to know!

Plane Shapes and Solids

1.
A plane shape lives on paper,
With dimensions only two.
A solid shape can be picked up
by her or him or you!

2.
A plane shape is a drawing
In pencil or in ink.
But a solid you can put things in,
Like an ice-cube in a drink.

3.
A polygon is a plane shape,
With straight sides three, or more.
A triangle has three straight sides,
A rectangle has four.

4.
A house-brick is a cuboid,
A die is a six-faced cube.
A tennis ball is called a sphere,
And a cylinder's a tube.

5.
So now you see the difference:
A solid you can throw.
A plane shape you can only draw,
That's all you need to know!

Octopus Tea

Maurice Walsh

1.
Ten little octopuses, eighty tentacles,
Swimming at the bottom of the crystal sea.
One little octopussy went back home
Because mum called her in for tea.
So that leaves…

2.
Nine little octopuses, seventy-two tentacles,
Swimming at the bottom of the crystal sea.
One little octopussy went back home
Because mum called her in for tea.
So that leaves…

3.
Eight little octopuses, sixty-four tentacles,
Swimming at the bottom of the crystal sea.
One little octopussy went back home
Because mum called her in for tea.
So that leaves…

4.
Seven little octopuses, fifty-six tentacles,
Swimming at the bottom of the crystal sea.
One little octopussy went back home
Because mum called her in for tea.
So that leaves…

OCTOPUS TEA — SUBTRACTION

5.
Six little octopuses, forty-eight tentacles,
Swimming at the bottom of the crystal sea.
One little octopussy went back home
Because mum called her in for tea.
So that leaves…

6.
Five little octopuses, forty tentacles,
Swimming at the bottom of the crystal sea.
One little octopussy went back home
Because mum called her in for tea.
So that leaves…

7.
Four little octopuses, thirty-two tentacles,
Swimming at the bottom of the crystal sea.
One little octopussy went back home
Because mum called her in for tea.
So that leaves…

8.
Three little octopuses, twenty-four
   tentacles,
Swimming at the bottom of the crystal sea.
One little octopussy went back home
Because mum called her in for tea.
So that leaves…

9.
Two little octopuses, sixteen tentacles,
Swimming at the bottom of the crystal sea.
One little octopussy went back home
Because mum called her in for tea.
So that leaves…

10.
One little octopus, just eight tentacles,
Swimming at the bottom of the crystal sea.
One little octopussy went back home
Because mum called her in for tea.

Octopus Tea

1.
Ten little octopuses, eighty tentacles,
Swimming at the bottom of the crystal sea.
One little octopussy went back home
Because mum called her in for tea.
So that leaves...

2.
Nine little octopuses, seventy-two tentacles,
Swimming at the bottom of the crystal sea.
One little octopussy went back home
Because mum called her in for tea.
So that leaves...

3.
Eight little octopuses, sixty-four tentacles,
Swimming at the bottom of the crystal sea.
One little octopussy went back home
Because mum called her in for tea.
So that leaves...

4.
Seven little octopuses, fifty-six tentacles,
Swimming at the bottom of the crystal sea.
One little octopussy went back home
Because mum called her in for tea.
So that leaves...

5.
Six little octopuses, forty-eight tentacles,
Swimming at the bottom of the crystal sea.
One little octopussy went back home
Because mum called her in for tea.
So that leaves...

6.
Five little octopuses, forty tentacles,
Swimming at the bottom of the crystal sea.
One little octopussy went back home
Because mum called her in for tea.
So that leaves...

7.
Four little octopuses, thirty-two tentacles,
Swimming at the bottom of the crystal sea.
One little octopussy went back home
Because mum called her in for tea.
So that leaves...

8.
Three little octopuses, twenty-four tentacles,
Swimming at the bottom of the crystal sea.
One little octopussy went back home
Because mum called her in for tea.
So that leaves...

9.
Two little octopuses, sixteen tentacles,
Swimming at the bottom of the crystal sea.
One little octopussy went back home
Because mum called her in for tea.
So that leaves...

10.
One little octopus, just eight tentacles,
Swimming at the bottom of the crystal sea.
One little octopussy went back home
Because mum called her in for tea.

TEN LITTLE CHILDREN   SUBTRACTION

Ten Little Children

Susan Eames

(In verses 3 to 9 do the pretends here)

Ten lit-tle chil-dren stand-ing in a line.

One goes off to do a job. *(One child walks away)* That leaves nine.

Last time only

That leaves none!

1.
Ten little children
Standing in a line.
One goes off to do a job.
That leaves nine.

2.
Nine little children
Standing up so straight.
One goes off to do a job.
That leaves eight.

3.
Eight little children
Pretend to write eleven.
One goes off to do a job.
That leaves seven.

4.
Seven little children
pretend to build with bricks.
One goes off to do a job.
That leaves six.

SUBTRACTION — TEN LITTLE CHILDREN

5.
Six little children
pretend they go to dive.
One goes off to do a job.
That leaves five.

6.
Five little children
Pretend to shut the door.
One goes off to do a job.
That leaves four.

7.
Four little children
Pretend to climb a tree.
One goes off to do a job.
That leaves three.

8.
Three little children
Pretend to stir some stew.
One goes off to do a job.
That leaves two.

9.
Two little children
Pretend to draw a sun.
One goes off to do a job.
That leaves one.

10.
One little child,
Our song is nearly done.
(He/she) goes off to do a job.
That leaves none.
That leaves none.

THE LITERACY AND NUMERACY SONG BOOK

Ten Little Children

1.
Ten little children
Standing in a line.
One goes off to do a job.
That leaves nine.

2.
Nine little children
Standing up so straight.
One goes off to do a job.
That leaves eight.

3.
Eight little children
Pretend to write eleven.
One goes off to do a job.
That leaves seven.

4.
Seven little children
pretend to build with bricks.
One goes off to do a job.
That leaves six.

5.
Six little children
pretend they go to dive.
One goes off to do a job.
That leaves five.

6.
Five little children
Pretend to shut the door.
One goes off to do a job.
That leaves four.

7.
Four little children
Pretend to climb a tree.
One goes off to do a job.
That leaves three.

8.
Three little children
Pretend to stir some stew.
One goes off to do a job.
That leaves two.

9.
Two little children
Pretend to draw a sun.
One goes off to do a job.
That leaves one.

10.
One little child,
Our song is nearly done.
He/she goes off to do a job.
That leaves none.
That leaves none.

The Clock Song

Clive Barnwell

1. Tick tock, tick tock, goes the ticking of the clock. Tick tock, tick tock, counting out the time. It never waits for any man, it's always rushing by. And I have heard some people say it's learning how to fly.

2. Tick tock, tick tock, it sometimes ticks and doesn't tock. Tick tock, tick tock, counting out the time. The minute hand moves quickly as it travels round the face. The hour hand moves gently at a slow and even pace.

THE CLOCK SONG

TIME

Chorus

What's the time now? Look at the clock. It's quarter past eleven and the chimes have struck.

There's just one thing wrong with our clock. It keeps on ticking nicely but the hands are stuck.

1.
2. & last time hands are stuck.
3. Each time the minute hand's at 12 the clock should strike its chimes. *Fine* The hour hand points the hour out to

TIME   THE CLOCK SONG

1.
Tick tock, tick tock
Goes the ticking of the clock.
Tick tock, tick tock,
Counting out the time.
It never waits for any man,
It's always rushing by.
And I have heard some people say
It's learning how to fly.

Chorus
What's the time now?
Look at the clock.
It's quarter past eleven and the chimes have struck.
There's just one thing
Wrong with our clock.
It keeps on ticking nicely but the hands are stuck.

2.
Tick tock, tick tock
It sometimes ticks and doesn't tock.
Tick tock, tick tock,
Counting out the time.
The minute hand moves quickly
As it travels round the face.
The hour hand moves gently
At a slow and even pace.

Chorus

3.
Each time the minute hand's at 12
The clock should strike its chimes.
The hour hand points the hour out
To say how many times.

Chorus

The Clock Song

1.
Tick tock, tick tock
Goes the ticking of the clock.
Tick tock, tick tock,
Counting out the time.
It never waits for any man,
It's always rushing by.
And I have heard some people say
It's learning how to fly.

Chorus
What's the time now?
Look at the clock.
It's quarter past eleven and the chimes have struck.
There's just one thing
Wrong with our clock.
It keeps on ticking nicely but the hands are stuck.

2.
Tick tock, tick tock
It sometimes ticks and doesn't tock.
Tick tock, tick tock,
Counting out the time.
The minute hand moves quickly
As it travels round the face.
The hour hand moves gently
At a slow and even pace.

Chorus

3.
Each time the minute hand's at 12
The clock should strike its chimes.
The hour hand points the hour out
To say how many times.

Chorus

Passing Time

Gerald Haigh

The mor-ning breaks, our house a-wakes, we share the day's first pot of tea. By half past eight, we're off to school, our Mam, our Sam and

1.
The morning breaks,
Our house awakes,
We share the day's first pot of tea.
By half past eight, we're off to school,
Our Mam, our Sam and me.

2.
We reach the gate,
We daren't be late.
I run inside and wave goodbye.
A wave from Mam, and one from Sam,
He'll miss me and he'll cry.

3.
We start at nine,
Stand in a line,
Then go inside to work in class.
It's usually easy, sometimes hard,
But working makes time pass.

4.
And then we all
Go in the hall
To eat our lunch at ten past noon.
I think of Mam, and think of Sam,
I'll see them both quite soon.

5.
At half past three,
They wait for me.
I get my coat and run outside,
And there is Mam, and little Sam,
Big smiles and arms spread wide.

6.
We're home by four,
Inside the door,
My turn to give our Sam his tea.
The day's gone by, it's bed by nine,
Quite late enough for me!

Passing Time

1.
The morning breaks,
Our house awakes,
We share the day's first pot of tea.
By half past eight, we're off to school,
Our Mam, our Sam and me.

2.
We reach the gate,
We daren't be late.
I run inside and wave goodbye.
A wave from Mam, and one from Sam,
He'll miss me and he'll cry.

3.
We start at nine,
Stand in a line,
Then go inside to work in class.
It's usually easy, sometimes hard,
But working makes time pass.

4.
And then we all
Go in the hall
To eat our lunch at ten past noon.
I think of Mam, and think of Sam,
I'll see them both quite soon.

5.
At half past three,
They wait for me.
I get my coat and run outside,
And there is Mam, and little Sam,
Big smiles and arms spread wide.

6.
We're home by four,
Inside the door,
My turn to give our Sam his tea.
The day's gone by, it's bed by nine,
Quite late enough for me!

Notes for Teachers

The Adjective Song (age 5–9)
You or the pupils might classify these adjectives – some are to do with appearance (with a sub-set of colours), some with characteristics. Where does 'young' fit in here – appearance, characteristic, or something else?

Adjectivally Me (age 5–9)
This song introduces a number of adjectives. You – or the pupils – could make a list of them. (How many are there? 21.) Look at the structure of some of them. 'Friendly' is an example of one that looks like an adverb, and is a warning against identifying adverbs by the 'ly' ending. Some are made from nouns – 'hopeful', 'contented' – and some are not. Discuss 'golden' which is an adjective made from the noun 'gold' – although it is a relic of an old construction and these days we might well use 'gold' as an adjective 'gold watch' is more common than 'golden watch'.

The Adverb Song (age 7–9)
This is about adverbs. There is much to say about the spelling rules that come into play – on 'energetically' for example, as opposed to 'dreamily'. Many are derived from adjectives, or nouns, or from both. Can you make a three-column list for each word – noun, adjective, adverb? Can you fill every column for every word? You can make your own verses – but consider whether your own adverbs will fit the rhythm of the line.

The Opposites Gang (age 5–7)
You can treat this as an 'echo' song – one group does 'I'm big', one does 'I'm small.' Don't have actual groups of small and big people, for obvious reasons, but the children could act out each characteristic – stretching for tall, shivering for cold, and so on.
You can tap or clap on the beat. You could make flash cards of the main words (or the word plus a picture if necessary) to be held up at the appropriate moment by you or the children.

A, E, I, O and U (age 7–9)
Discuss why vowels are important – there are, for all practical purposes, no English words without vowels. Discuss the effect of doubling vowels – oo, ee. Can other vowels be doubled in English? Letters which are not vowels are consonants. Discuss the ambiguity of Y. This song presents the option of including Y as a vowel. Choose whether you want to do this. The CD provides both versions.

I Love Those Fairy Tales (age 5–9)
Think of the bass of the piano part as giant footsteps – if you put a good accent, as indicated, on the last note of each bar in the introduction, it will give you the idea.
You could make a class list of books that fit the mood of the song.

When I Look in a Book (age 5–9)
This could be a 'favourite book' song, with children bringing a favourite book out to the front as the song is sung. Used in this way it could become an enjoyable routine each week.

Read All About It! (age 7–9)
This is about what's in a newspaper. Using newspapers, children can find the various elements mentioned in the song – TV guide, fashion, world news and so on. Is anything missing from any paper?

Fact or Opinion? (age 9–11)
The difference between fact and opinion is often quite subtle. Discuss this, perhaps in relation to the school. 'This is a primary school' – fact. 'This is a good school' – is that a fact or an opinion? Can it ever be a fact? What evidence might confirm it as a fact? Historians know that 'facts' are rarely as cut

THE LITERACY AND NUMERACY SONG BOOK

and dried as we would like them to be. Discuss the challenge to the poet of finding rhymes for 'opinion'. Is 'million', for example, a true rhyme? How far into a word, as it were, does the rhyme have to extend? Do the children have any offers for rhymes with 'opinion'?

Magic E (age 5–9)
Is there a magic E at work in other parts of the song? You can find it in 'makes' and 'name'.
Look at the line 'It's magic, can't you see?'. There's a problem for singers here – the same consonant at the end of one word and the beginning of the next. Discuss this. In casual speech or song you would often just say the 'c' once. But good choral or singing technique is to say both consonants, with a tiny break between. Helping the children to do this will concentrate their minds on the words and how to say them.

Look, Cover, Write and Check It (age 5–9)
This is an effective help to learning spellings. You can try making 'paper teachers'. A paper teacher is a piece of paper folded into three columns. You write the word in the left-hand column. The child copies the word in the middle column, then folds the left column over to cover the middle column, and finally writes the word from memory in the right-hand column. Open the paper teacher to check that all three words are the same.

I Before E (age 5–9)
Are there any exceptions to this rule? What other spelling rules can you and the children write down? What about a double consonant shortening the previous vowel – 'shinning up to reach the shining lamp.'

A Sound Song (age 5–9)
This bouncy little song is about the spelling of words with 'ough', 'ight', 'tion' and 'eigh'.

The H Song (age 5–7)
This is about the effect of adding 'h' to various consonants to make the blends 'ch' 'th' and so on.

Puss in Boots Rap (age 5–7)
A rap is rhythmic speech. Don't be put off by the notation – it's there to help and to sort out any problems. And, of course, it would be a good teaching aid if you were covering notation in a music lesson. Apart from that, start by relying on the natural rhythm of the words, checking with the notation as you need. The CD has an accompaniment with added percussion which the pupils will undoubtedly enjoy.

Apostrophes (age 7–9)
This song needs supporting with some illustrations of correct and incorrect use of apostrophes.

Do They Ride into the Sun? (age 7–9)
This is about endings. Discuss the idea that an idea for a good ending might well be the inspiration for a whole story – and perhaps develop this in a writing lesson.

Punctuation Signs (age 7–9)
Show big graphic examples of each punctuation mark as the song is sung, and/or get the children to make the shape of the marks with their hands at the end of each verse before the chorus.

The Writing's on the Wall (age 7–9)
A celebration of writing, not requiring too much analysis. The quotation, though – 'The pen is mightier than the sword' – makes a good discussion point.

Similes (age 7–9)
There are lots of examples of similes in this song, to reinforce the concept. Pupils could add their own.

Capital Letter Blues (age 5–9)
Important to get the 'blues' feel in this. If you're not sure, listen to some slow jazz. The song moves through keys. You could do it all in the key of the first verse, but try to do the key changes if you possibly can. There are lots of opportunities for adding and changing verses.
Can you find examples that break the capital

letter rules? In e-mail addresses, for example, and often on letterheads and advertising material. Are such examples in any sense wrong?

Dinosaurs (age 4–7)
This is about doubling numbers – square numbers in fact, a theme which could be developed if the children are ready for it. In performance, get louder and softer as the dinosaurs. This could be done just by singing louder and softer, or by adding and taking away groups of singers as the song goes on. Use simple percussion to keep the beat.

Ten Fat Caterpillars (age 5–7)
This song has number bonds to ten, and also the concepts of 'on top' and 'underneath'. You can make a cabbage leaf and ten caterpillars from card, stuck on with Blu-tak, and moving them as the song goes on. Or – a bit more complicated – you could have a metal tray and caterpillars with magnets. (Make sure the tray is the right metal, though!)

Cutting Corners (age 7–9)
This is reinforcement of the concept of the right-angled triangle. The song incorporates an activity, which would be done separately, but could perhaps eventually be done as the song is sung. The second verse goes on to look at the names of different kinds of triangles.

One Knock at the Door (age 5–7)
Obviously you need to do the knocks, either with percussion or with taps on a desk. You can divide the song up among groups or individuals doing alternate lines or phrases.

Cornucopia (age 7–9)
Discuss the title – look up the meaning. How does it relate to the content of the song? The song is really a feast of descriptive words. There are things to say about adjectives and adverbs here – but don't overdo this. Just enjoy the language and the tune.

Count Your Fingers (age 4–7)
A deliberately simple song for young children – but older ones will enjoy joining in and doing the actions. The leader need not always be the teacher.

Sausage Boogie (age 7–9)
This shows that division is actually repeated subtraction. As well as just enjoying the song, you can use it for mental arithmetic by stopping after verses four and five to check how many sausages have gone and how many are left. Finally, you can write out the division sum at the end.
Other teaching points: the song is a twelve-bar blues – a common form in popular music. There are a number of versions, this is a simple one – four bars of F, two of B flat, two of F, one of C, one of B flat, two of F. It has to go with a bouncy jazz feel. The piano riff can be used as you like – perhaps to keep the mood while you do the mental arithmetic. If you can do the chord changes, it will also work as an accompaniment. On the CD the piano riff is inserted between the verses.

Sharing (age 5–7)
Use real pots with pencils and do the actions as you sing the song. If you like, cover up the answer on the OHP so the children can work it out. You can also do the same song with different numbers of pencils and pots.

Twenty-Four Pieces – Wow! (age 5–7)
Sharing chocolate – to support the idea of division. You could write the maths down to illustrate it; you could act out the various transactions with counters or real chocolate!

Peter Metre Eater (age 5–7)
Use a metre rule and measure out a metre stride – quite a big step for a child – and, if there's room, children will have fun trying to do metre strides.
You could discuss the word 'metre' and the fact that it rhymes with 'Peter'.

Multiplication March (age 7–9)
Think American Army marching song here – call and response. The leader can be the teacher, another pupil, a group of pupils, or any combination. (The name 'Lou' is double gender.) It's easy to think of other verses,

THE LITERACY AND NUMERACY SONG BOOK

and pupils will enjoy doing this – start with a multiplication fact and work back to the rhyming line. Three figure answers are spelled out – 'eleven elevens are one two one.'

Soldiers Marching (age 5–7)
Do the sums with fingers – two fists outstretched, two little fingers up for the first sum, then two on each hand and so on.

The Seven Times Table Song (age 7–9)
The 'answers' – 'Seven', 'Fourteen' and so on – could be solos. A child can volunteer to stand out at the front and do the answers while the class sings the rest of the song. Or, if the teacher writes up the table first, without answers, there's just time to write each answer as the song goes on.

Number Blues (age 5–7)
Get the blues feel into this, without worrying too much about the notated timing. You could do more verses – as many as you like really.

Day without Numbers (age 5–9)
This song can be extended, with lots of other situations and examples. It might also spark off ideas for stories in a writing lesson.

Clementine (age 5–7)
Draw Clementine and work out ways of grouping and counting her feet – in twos, in fours, in fives.

Up, Down, Round About (age 5–7)
These 'position' words are important in early mathematical understanding and the more practice young children have the better. Do the actions – with hand movements, or walking and moving on the spot or, in the hall, with more extended walking and movement. In this latter case, the song could be used, for example, to finish off a PE lesson.

Sir Cumference (age 7–9)
You will need an illustration showing all the examples on a circle. Discuss the relationships between them.

Symmetry (age 7–9)
The symmetry is in the tune. If you play it backwards it is exactly the same. The children can see this in the notation even if they are not yet entirely familiar with notation.

Plane Shapes and Solids (age 5–7)
A plane shape is abstract in the sense that it is two dimensional and can only exist as a representation on a flat surface. Solids, though, can be real objects. Examine the relationship between plane shapes and solids – put solids on the OHP to see them as plane shapes of different kinds. Make 'nets' which can convert plane shapes into solids.

Octopus Tea (age 5–7)
This is the eight times table. You could illustrate it with pictures of octopuses. There are suggestions for other animals with different numbers of limbs.

Ten Little Children (age 5–7)
Counting down from ten. Have ten children standing side by side in a line. There is space in the music for the children to mime the pretend actions and for one child to walk away from the line in each verse.

The Clock Song (age 5–9)
You could do this with a big model clock on hand to show the times.

Passing Time (age 5–7)
This is intended to be quite dreamy – a reflective mood about the passing of time during the day, as a child thinks about home and her little brother.